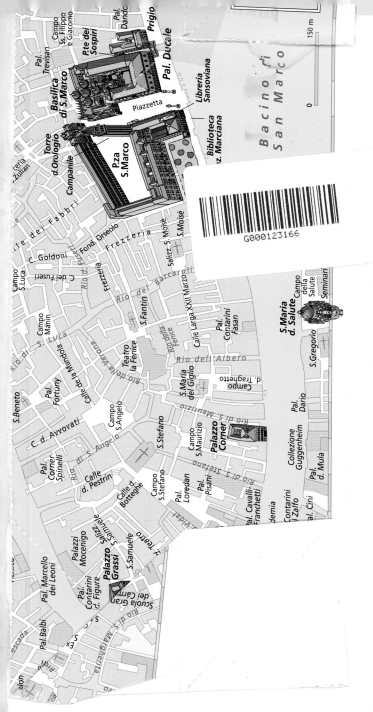

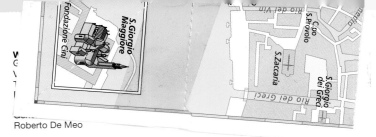

Roberto De Meo

Editor
Christiane Splinter

Text
Cesare Urbani

Picture research
Cristina Reggioli

Editing
Chiara Berti

Layout & graphics
Media Studio, Firenze

English edition
Roberta Anderson, Angela Arnone

Cover
Rocío Isabel González

Maps
Sergio Biagi, Firenze

Updating
Barbara Orlandini

The publisher cannot be held liable for damages or
problems arising from errors or information in this guide
book. Since many data and much information is subject
to change, we advise readers to verify in advance.

Unless otherwise indicated, images are part of Giunti
Archive. The publisher will settle any reproduction rights for
images that are not drawn from
the abovementioned source.

www.giunti.it

© 2005, Giunti Editore S.p.A.
Via Bolognese 165, - 50139 Firenze - Italia
Via Dante, 4 - 20121 Milano - Italia
Updated edition: 2007

Reprint	Year
5 4 3 2 1 0	2011 2010 2009 2008 2007

Printed in China

Weekend in...
Venice

TABLE OF CONTENTS

Presentation

"The flat coast showed on the right, the sea was soon populous with fishing-boats. The Lido appeared and was left behind as the ship glided at half speed through the narrow harbour ...

(1)

He saw it once more, that landing-place that takes the breath away, that amazing group of incredible structures the Republic set up to meet the awe-struck eye of the approaching seafarer: the airy splendour of the palace and the Bridge of Sighs, the columns of lion and saint on the shore, the glory of the projecting flank of the fairy temple, the vista of gateway and clock.

Looking, he thought that to come to Venice by the station is like entering a palace by the back door. No one should approach, save by the high seas as he was doing now, this most improbable of cities."

This is how Thomas Mann described the arrival of Gustav von Aschenbach in La Serenissima in "Death in Venice" (1911) (1).

In the early 20th century the city's commercial power had waned but it was able to seduce its visitors with a succession of churches, palazzi, schools of exceptional architectural value; with frescoes, sculptures and canvases that are the keystone of Italian art; with the charm of its tiny squares and lanes where time seems to have stood still since the golden age of the 15th and 16th centuries. What remains of this charm, so exceptional that Lord Byron wrote "those days are gone, but Beauty is still here"? A great deal, despite the daily risk that mass tourism will suffocate it as thousands upon thousands of trippers arrive to "see" it in just one day (2). We must find a way to see past this blatantly touristy aspect and seek to distance ourselves from the massive crowd that at certain times of day transforms Piazza San Marco into a bivouac that slows progress to snail's pace along Riva degli Schiavoni or Le Mercerie, in the direction of the Rialto Bridge. At some times of year this is objectively a difficult task, but not impossible. The effort will be well compensated by the profound silences of Castello Island, the breathtaking views from Le Zattere across La Giudecca, the sophisticated milieu of Ca' Rezzonico or the masterpieces in the Galleria Giorgio Franchetti. Not to mention San Marco and La Salute, the Accademia Galleries and the Schools of San Rocco and San Giorgio degli Schiavoni. Early in the morning, perhaps, or in the late afternoon, when the Venetians peek out onto the lanes once more.

(2)

The Lady of the Mediterranean

The Origins

The discovery of Roman craft shipwrecked in the lagoon and sea opposite the Lido confirms that the area where Venice was founded was already frequented at least in Imperial times, although the chief colonies of that era were on the coast and in many cases could boast Paleoveneto foundation. It was after the fall of the Western Roman Empire under the terrible blows inflicted by the barbarians that the inhabitants of some districts took refuge on the nearby islands, surrounded by water and thereby safer: this was the origin of Torcello, "embryonic" Venice, flourishing and wealthy from the 5th to the 10th century, but in decline after the northern sector of the lagoon turned into a swamp. The birth of Venice can be dat-

ed to the 9th century. There were several factors that made it possible: a bishop was installed on the island of Castello, documented in 775; the presence of a lay authority is documented from at least 810; but above all the arrival in the Lagoon of the remains of St Mark the Evangelist, stolen from Alexandria in 828 by two merchants, and stored in a chapel of the Palazzo Ducale of that time **(3)**.

The Evolution of Venice

The city's development under the trade aspect is attributable to the bishop-doge duo: the pair fostered the opening and organization of a port for landing merchandise arriving in the West from the Orient. This was a far-sighted policy since La Serenissima played a starring role from the 10th to 11th century in trade between the Eastern Roman Empire and the Holy Roman Empire, re-established by Charlemagne, exercising control over the Adriatic coast (so a condensed form of a "maritime state" was already present). Another key moment for the city was the decision to take part in the first crusade (1096). It was a forced decision, given the

(4)

rivalry between the feuding cities of Genoa and Pisa; a choice that proved to be successful from many points of view, since the capture of Jerusalem (1099) led to the establishment of trade relations with Acre (1110) and Tyre (1124) **(4)**.

From the Crusades to the Wars against Genoa

The opportunity to rely on transit ports in the Middle East was a turning point for Venice; this supremacy roused the ire of Byzantium and lead to the arrest of Venetian merchants in 1171. Yet the Lagoon settlement must have enjoyed significant importance at continental level: first (1177) it was actually chosen as the location for a European peace congress; then (1192) it became the point of departure for the fourth crusade. The city played a vital role in this venture (Constantinople was taken mainly thanks to the doges' fleet) and, in return for the establishment of the Latin Empire (1205), it acquired part of Byzantine possessions

(3)

(1)

almost all its possession in just a few years, but in 1517 it relinquished any further inland expansion on the peninsula and concentrated on the Turkish peril: Ottoman expansionism was only temporarily halted by the famous Battle of Lepanto (7 October 1571), where 230 Turkish warships were defeated by 208 Christian vessels (of which more than half were Venetian).

Decline and Fall of La Serenissima

In the early 17th century, Venice was still trade leader with the Orient, but it was only a question of time before the Turks raised their heads. In fact, the second half of the century was marked by a series of retreats by La Serenissima, which culminated in 1666 with an attack on Crete that was definitively abandoned in 1671. It is true that precisely in that period the Doge Francesco Morosini (2) managed to conquer much of the Greek Peloponnesus (1687); but the

(Corfu, 1207; Crete, 1209). When Constantinople was freed (1261), the conflict between Venice and Genoa was inevitable, marking the 14th century, initially in parallel with the battles in defence of the Muslim threat to the strongholds in Palestine, and then with attempts to expand the Italian signories: the Ligurian city conquered Chioggia in 1381; at the same time part of the Adriatic's eastern coasts were taken by Hungary.

The Golden Age
The solidity of Venetian political structures is evident from its ability to push back the Hungarian assault. Alliance and counteroffensive politics brought under the direct control of the city not only several Eastern Mediterranean islands (Corfu as well as Kephalonia and Cyprus), but also Euboea, whilst the close existing trade links enabled the submission of Treviso,

Padua, Vicenza and Verona, initiating that "stato de tera" or "land state" that earned Venice the name of "The Dominator" (1462) and a frontline role in Italian and European affairs. 1494 was another important date in the city's history: the French Emperor Charles VIII descended on Italy and the Turks, who conquered Constantinople in 1453, began their attack of Venice's oriental stations. The doges applied politics that managed to avoid foreign dominion of La Serenissima, but also conceived the unfortunate venture of extending the "land state", damaging the Church; hence the foundation of the League of Cambrai (in 1508 Austria, France and Spain formed an alliance against Venice (1)) and the defeat at Agnadello (1509), which appeared to curtail the success of The Dominator. Nevertheless, the city succeeded in recovering

(2)

courageous exploit did not halt the Passarovitz Treaty (1718) that reduced Venetian holdings to just the Adriatic. In less than 80 years the last of the doges, Ludovico Manin (3), handed the city and its land and sea holdings to an overseas power: on 15 May 1797 the sun finally set on The Dominator by order of Napoleon.

(4)

(3)

Seeking a new role

Neither the French government (1797-1815) nor the Austrian (1815-66) were able to outline a new future or a different role for Venice. Both states, however, transformed the city's layout, both in its links with the land and in the enhancement of its port. This was continued after the Unification of Italy (19 October 1866), in an attempt to ensure that the marvellous monumental heritage would cohabit with progress. So the invention of the International Art Biennale (1895) was intended as a sort of tribute to the city's role in a cultural context (4) and

the Film Festival (1930s) was the ideal method for connecting with the Lido's high society glamour as a seaside resort for Central Europe (5), the opening of Marghera industrial district (1917) forced on Venice a vocation with which it was unfamiliar. The decision to annex the city with the Mestre area (1927) simply endorsed a split in the city's appearance: the ancient nucleus clinging to a noble glorious past, expansion on dry land heading for a productive future. This decision was shown to be a failure, both for the environmental devastation brought to the Lagoon by the in-

dustrial plants and for the progressive museumification of the historic centre. This is precisely the most serious risk that the city runs, in these early years of the third millennium, far more dramatic than the high tides that flood it with increasing frequency: due to pressing tourist demands on one hand, and the prohibitive cost of maintaining homes on the other, employment opportunities that do not involve tourism and trade are virtually non-existent, (despite the prestigious Universities and cultural institutions), and residents have fled en masse.

(5)

Useful information

Climate

Clear days on the Lagoon can be counted on the fingers of one hand and correspond to moments when the bora or fall wind blows, making the silhouettes of the is-

lands on the horizon and the city's monumental skyline as sharp as can be. Days of fog and rain are as numerous as ever, so Venice's fame as a damp city does not falter. Summer months are often very hot.

When to visit

As Venice is one of the capitals of Italian and international tourism, there is really no "low season", for those who would prefer to walk the city as a Venetian does, or take a solitary stroll. Nowadays it is difficult to recommend a good moment for a visit. Carnival and important religious feast days are particularly crowded, as are the Film Festival and, on alternate years, the Art Biennale. If fog and rain do not deter you, then November and January are ideal; if you are immune

to heat and mosquitoes, then July can offer some pleasant surprises.

By car

After the inauguration of the bridge over the Lagoon (1933), even the only traffic-free city in Italy could be reached by road. Certainly it is not the most convenient way, but there are plenty of tourists who do decide to do it this way, arriving at Venice on the A4 Turin-Trieste motorway (Mestre exit). You can then leave your car behind, parking it at the lots in Piazzale Roma and on the islands of Tronchetto and San Giuliano, or even in Mestre.

By train

This is the best way to reach La Serenissima, since the

Italian State Railways *(information from the site: www.trenitalia.it)* ensure hourly connections on the Turin-Milan, Trieste and Bologna-Rome lines.

By air

The "Marco Polo" airport at Venice Tessera *(information: 0412609260)* is one of Italy's busiest. It is on the mainland north of the city, but is connected to the centre by the city bus no. 5 (every 30 minutes), by a shuttle service (leaving every 30 minutes), by taxi overland (stopping at Piazzale Roma) and by water taxi across the northern part of the Lagoon.

Events

If you want to combine your trip to Venice with one of the religious or lay events for which the city is famous, here is a list of the main dates: Carnival (Jan.-Feb.); Feast of

St Mark (25 April); Feast of La Sensa (Ascension); May); Art Biennale (June every two years); Feast of the Redeemer (third weekend in July); Film Festival (late August-early September); Historic Regatta (first Sunday in September); Feast of Our Lady of Health (21 Nov.). The list is completed by sports events like the famous Vogalonga rowing event (May) and the Venice Marathon (last Sunday in October).

Useful numbers

Garage Comunale, p.le Roma, tel. 0412727301, www.asmvenezia.it; *Garage Sant'Andrea,* p.le Roma, tel. 0412727304; *Parking Stazione,* v.le Stazione 10, Mestre, tel. 041938021. *Garage San Marco*, p.le Roma, tel. 0415232213; fax 0415289969 www.garagesanmarco.it *Green Park*, via Righi 3, Porto Marghera, tel. 0415317315 *Terminal Service*, via dei Petroli 3, Porto Marghera, tel. 0415317917 *Toderini*, p.le Roma, tel. 0415207979. *Venezia Tronchetto Parking*, Tronchetto, tel. 0415207555; fax 0415285750; www.veniceparking.it

Information

Azienda Promozione Turistica, Castello 5050, tel. 0415298700; fax 0415230399; www.turismovenezia.it *Hello Venezia*, tel. 0412424 www.hellovenezia.it *Information offices*:
- S. Marco 71/f;
- Palazzina dei Santi (ex Giardini reali);
- Venice Santa Lucia Railway Station;
- ASM Municipal garage parking, Piazzale Roma;
- Marco Polo airport (arrivals hall).

Discount Card

The Venice Card (*www.venicecard.it*) is a single ticket for the most important services in the city. Visitors can choose between the Venice Blue Card, including public transport and toilettes, and the Venice Orange Card, which also includes the city's Municipal Museums.

Taxi

In Venice taxi services are run by motor boats; authorized taxis have a yellow stripe and black numbering.

Public transport

Venice Transport Consortium (ACTV) manages a multiform transport network, which includes water-buses [vaporetto], buses and ferries connecting the island of Tronchetto and the Lido. The former run along the central backbone of the Canal Grande, but ensure connections with the islands; the latter serve the municipality's inland suburbs and the Lido. There are various types of tickets, but unless you are a tireless walker it is worthwhile picking up a multiple day

pass, which often offers discounts on tickets to various museums. If money is no problem, a ride in a gondola is still a very romantic way to discover the city. Finally, since there are only three bridges that cross Canal Grande, there is a gondola-ferry service between the two banks of Venice's chief thoroughfare, with quite extensive schedules.

FROM PIAZZA SAN

*H*owever often you go to visit Venice, it is difficult to resist the temptation to gaze over Piazza San Marco and admire its unique backdrop of buildings or stroll along Riva degli Schiavoni, letting your mind wander back in time to the era of the glorious Dominator.

KEY

1. Piazza S. Marco
2. Basilica di S. Marco
3. Torre dell'Orologio
4. Procuratie Vecchie e Nuove
5. Museo Correr
6. Museo Archeologico
7. Campanile di S. Marco
8. Libreria Sansoviniana
9. Biblioteca Nazionale Marciana
10. Piazzetta S. Marco
11. Palazzo Ducale
12. Riva degli Schiavoni
13. S. Zaccaria
14. S. Giovanni in Bragora
15. Arsenale
16. Museo Storico Navale
17. Giardini Pubblici
18. S. Pietro di Castello

MARCO TO CASTELLO

Best done early in the morning, when the basilica parvis is occupied only by pigeons and real Venetians will be found making their way along the San Marco basin towards San Pietro di Castello.

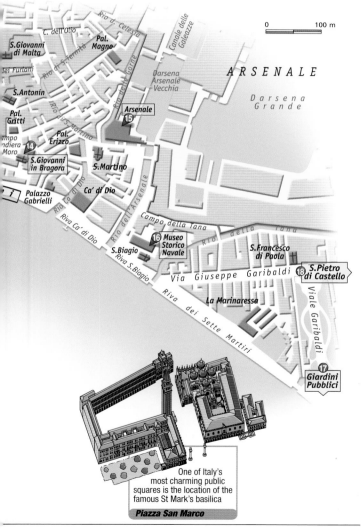

One of Italy's most charming public squares is the location of the famous St Mark's basilica

Piazza San Marco

(1)

1. Piazza S. Marco

Emblem of La Serenissima worldwide and one of Italy's most magical public areas and actually Venice's only square **(1)**. At the dawn of the city's history, it was a garden crossed by a canal, but its destiny was changed following the building of the basilica dedicated to St Mark, for which the piazza is now an enormous parvis. The first part to be built was the Procuratie Vecchie, to the north, and in the 15th-16th century – as part of Sansovino's project for the reorganization of the area – the Procuratie Nuove, to the south, as well as the Libreria Sansoviniana, which connects the square to Piazzetta San Marco. The French government then completed (19th century) this backdrop of buildings by joining the two Procuratie with the Napoleonic Wing.

2. Basilica di San Marco
Mon.-Sat. 9.45-16.45; Sun. 14-16.30

If Piazza San Marco is the quintessence of a public area in the city, the most famous building is the basilica erected following the arrival of the remains of St Mark the Evangelist from Alexandria (828). It was commissioned by the Doge Giustiniano Partecipazio but the building we see today is dated 1060, when the basilica was rebuilt following a fire: it was then that the Greek cross plan was adopted, with four small cupolas that surround the central, larger dome and creation of the mosaics, which continued for many centuries. In the 13th century the domes were covered with lead sheet and acquired their unique bowl appearance, whilst from the 14th to the 16th century, the atrium was transformed in part into the baptistery and in part into the Zen chapel. The sobriquet "golden basilica" is easily understood even from the exterior: the façade on Piazza San Marco, divided into two levels by a balcony broken at the centre by copies of the horses **(2)** from the famous bronze quadriga (the originals are in the Marciano Museum, inside the basilica) actually offers a hint in the portal lunettes of the artistic mosaic that glows within (the only ancient part – 1260-70 – is the mosaic on the first left-hand arch). The Romanesque bas-reliefs (13th century) in the central and main arch are, however, quite precious. The basilica's southern façade is bound to the neighbouring Palazzo Ducale by the famous group of the Tetrarchs **(3)**, thought to be 4th century, depicting Diocletian and the

(2)

other Emperors who governed Roman dominions with him; the prospect's facing vertex englobes the "pietra del bando", a truncated column from which La Serenissima's public laws and notices were announced. The actual interior of the basilica is preceded by an atrium, opened after 1094, with a bay structure covered by false cupolas; the mosaics

(4)

(3)

are the most interesting decorative element, created by 12th-13th century Venetian artists and depicting episodes from the *Old Testament* (4); the most significant are the 24 episodes of *Genesis*, the stories of Abel and Cain (cupola in the first bay; 1230 circa), as well as the even more historic (11th century) *Madonna, Saints* and *Evangelists* (second bay). The interior of the church retains its Byzantine plan, with cupolas supported by pillars and columns with marvellous capitals: the nave extends beyond

the transept, into the presbytery, which is raised by an underlying crypt, and is paved, as are the aisles, by multicoloured marble mosaics. Only a few of the mosaics that cover much of the interior are 12th-14th century: the *Passion* scenes, in the intrados between the first and second cupolas in the nave, date back to the 13th century, and the mosaics in the Ascension cupola at the crossing and those on the right transept wall are of the same period. The transept is separated from the presbytery by a mul-

ticoloured marble iconostasis decorated with statues (1396), some by Jacobello and Pier Paolo dalle Masegne; the Prophet mosaics in the cupola that closes the upper part of the presbytery are dated 12th century, and it is here, behind the high altar, that you will find the **Pala d'Oro (5)**, a magnificent altarpiece that is a masterpiece of Byzantine goldsmithing commissioned by Doge Pietro Orseolo I in the late 10th and completed in the 14th century (it includes 1,300 pearls, 400 garnets, 300 sapphires and emeralds, 90 amethysts, 80 enamels, 75 balas-rubies, 15 rubies, 4 topazes and 2 cameos). The *Nicopeia* or *Odegitria* Madonna (the Madonna who brings victory or leadership, 11th-13th century), said to have been brought from Constantinople as booty from the Fourth Crusade, is in the left-hand transept, where part of the lunette and

(5)

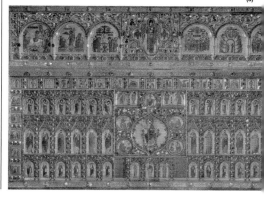

(2)

intrados mosaics are early 13th century. Those in the Sant'Isidoro chapel are Late Romanesque and still influenced by the Ravenna style, whereas those in the neighbouring Madonna dei Mascoli chapel document the evolution from Gothic to Renaissance. The aisles are also covered in mosaics; *Jesus praying in the Garden* (1220; right-hand aisle) is impressive, as is the *Virgin in prayer with the Prophets* (1250 c.; left-hand aisle).

(1)

St Mark's Treasure
Mon.-Sat. 9.45-16.45; Sun. 14-16.45

The aisle on the right of the transept leads to the Basilica's Treasure, which was initiated by the enormous booty brought back to the city from the Fourth Crusade; the 283 items on show are "what re-

mains" after serious pillaging perpetrated by Napoleon's government during the 18th and 19th centuries: a corpus of inestimable value, including significant Byzantine productions (reliquaries) (1).

Marciano Museum
9.45-16.45

The original horses of the bronze quadriga have been in the museum since the 1880s: they are of uncertain date (some say they are 4th century, of the period of Constantine, others say they are Greek and of the 4th-3rd century BC) and origin, standing out in the context of bronze statuary for their exceptional elegance and vigorous expression.

Another masterpiece on display here is the so-called "pala feriale" altarpiece (2), painted in 1345 by Paolo Veneziano, intended to substitute the "pala d'Oro" when it was not on display.

3. Torre dell'Orologio

The Moors whose hammers strike out the hours on the bell are located on a terrace at the top of the Clock Tower (Torre dell'Orologio), built in the late 15th century by Mauro Codussi on the left of the basilica (3). It is surprising to note how advanced mechanical knowledge was even at that time. In fact, the face, embellished with gilding and blue enamel, not only tells the time, but is also a sundial with signs of the zodiac and lunar phases, while during Ascension Week the Magi emerge

(3)

(4)

from the left-hand door and bow to the *Madonna and Child* above.

4. Procuratie Vecchie and Nuove

The old and new residences of the Procurator of St Mark's extend from the clock tower, documented as early as the 12th century, but were rebuilt in their current style in the 16th century, and one of Venice's most famous historic locations, the **Caffè Quadri**, is installed under their arcades. The neoclassical-style Ala Napoleonica, which closes Piazza San Marco to the west, was erected early in the 19th century as a trait-d'union with the Procuratie Nuove, which were also lightened by a ground floor arcade, housing another historic meeting place, the **Caffè Florian (4)**, but designed by Sansovino and completed in the 17th century by Baldassarre Longhena.

5. Museo Correr

April-Oct., Wed.-Mon. 9-19; Nov.-March, Wed.-Mon. 9-17

The neoclassical stairway beneath the Ala Napoleonica arcade leads to the collections assembled by the nobleman Teodoro Correr and given by him to the city; over time the collections have grown and illustrate the city's history and Venetian culture with a multifaceted range of items that include, significantly, works by Antonio Canova and the Correr and Morosini armouries. The building's upper storey is a picture gallery that illustrates local production from its origins to the early 16th century: prominent pieces include a *Pietà* by Cosmè Tura (1468 c.) and another by Antonello da Messina (1476), a *Crucifixion* by

(5)

Jacopo Bellini (post-1450), a *Madonna and Child* **(5)** by Giovanni Bellini (1460-64) and Carpaccio's *Venetian Ladies* (1510-15).

6. Museo Archeologico

9-20

The multiple "Percorso Marciano" ticket gives entry to the Archaeological Museum from the Correr Museum. The Archaeological Museum was established using the 16th-century collections of Cardinal Domenico Grimani and it was enhanced by legacies left, in part, by his successors **(6)**. This explains the wide timescale covered by the exhibits,

(6)

which include several Egyptian examples alongside Assyrian-Babylonian and Roman items; the most interesting section is that of the statues, which has countless originals of the archaic era.

7. Campanile di San Marco

Oct.-March β9.45-16; Apr.-June 9.30-17; July-Sept. 9.45-20

To enjoy 360-degree view over the city, as far as the Euganei Hills on clear days, simply climb to the top of "el paron de casa". The "landlord", as the Venetians call the San Marco belfry, is another symbolic monument of

15

(1)

legion of *Wisdom* (1564); the room is hallmarked by its equilibrium and elegance, which Sansovino in person ordered to be decorated with paintings of philosophers by Paolo Veronese, Andrea Schiavone and Tintoretto, and which also houses Fra Mauro's impressive globe (15th century).

9. Biblioteca Nazionale Marciana

April-Sep., Mon.-Fri. 9-19, Sat. 9-14; Oct.-March, Mon.-Fri. 9-17, Sat. 9-13

In the instructions given to Sansovino for building the Libreria Sansoviniana, this was for the Marciana National Library. Since 1904, however, this institution occupies another building also designed and erected by the Florentine Sansovino: Palazzo della Zecca, which faces out onto the San Marco basin, with a façade split into a ground floor arcade and two floors cadenced by columns that are respectively Doric and Ionic. The inner courtyard, transformed into a reading room, has been roofed with a skylight; the most

(2)

valuable item is the **Grimani breviary (2)**, a codex of 831 sheets illuminated by 15th-16th century Flemish artists.

10. Piazzetta S. Marco

At one time the façades of the Libreria Sansoviniana and Palazzo Ducale gleamed in the waters of the San Marco basin, and the Lagoon waves lapped the walls of St Mark's basilica (3). The area was then filled in to create Piazzetta San Marco, whose water front is decorated with the columns of St Mark and St Todaro, both brought from the Orient in the 12th century, each bearing a statue of La Serenissima's two patron saints: St Mark stands on

this city, built in the 9th century as a watchtower then refurbished early in the 16th century. What you see nowadays, however, is the result of a reconstruction "as it was and where it was", undertaken following its sudden collapse on 14 July 1902. At that time a reintegration was also made of the "Loggetta" that in 1537-49 Sansovino had set against the side of the belfry facing the basilica (1).

8. Libreria Sansoviniana

Mon.-Fri. 9-19; Sat. 9-19.30

A magnificent example of Renaissance architecture, the library was designed – in the project for the rearrangement of Piazza San Marco – and begun by Sansovino, who took his inspiration from the Procuratie Vecchie for the dual-order (Doric and Ionic) external prospect with underlying arcade. Here two caryatids guard the access to the building and beyond them a monumental, two-ramp staircase decorated with stuccoes rises to the vestibule, embellished with Titian's Al-

(3)

the column nearest to Palazzo Ducale; Todaro (St Theodore, lost his role in the 9th century) stands on the column nearest the Libreria Sansoviniana.

11. Palazzo Ducale

Apr.-Oct. 9-19; Nov.-Mar. 9-17

Politically and commercially the Golden Age of La Serenissima was written within this building, with one prospect closing the eastern side of Piazzetta San Marco and another mirrored by the waters of the Lagoon (4). What is considered the masterpiece of Venetian Gothic architecture was built in the 9th century as a castle (it was already the residence of the Doge, moved there from Malamocco) and it was rebuilt in Venetian-Byzantine style (12th century), with a series of extensions and refurbishments undertaken from the 14th to the 17th

(4)

century. The two prospects are identical: two full-centre arches serve as a continuous loggia – with a double number of arches and quatrefoiled apertures – as well as a solid wall with the hallmark lozenge design, topped by crenellations; the balconies, which break up the upper section alongside the windows, are respectively by Antonio Scarpagnino and Sansovino (16th century; Piazzetta San Marco) and Jacobello and Pier Paolo dalle Masegne (15th cen-

tury; San Marco basin). Beyond the 15th-century Carta door, between the basilica and the portico, and Gothic Foscari arch, there is a courtyard on the right, closed by a sequence of porches on loggias that date back to the 14th-17th centuries, and opposite there is the splendid Giganti staircase (15th-16th century), decorated with statues by Sansovino, who also designed the **scala d'Oro** staircase **(5)**, thus known for its stuccoed vault, which marks the actual entrance to the interior of Palazzo Ducale. First it serves the Ducal Apartments, rebuilt after a blaze in 1483 and stripped of all its

(5)

Palladio's masterpiece

However clichéd it may have become, the view of the island of San Giorgio Maggiore and its church from Piazzetta San Marco, is still breathtaking. The scrap of land, a stone's throw from the San Marco area, owes its magnificent appearance (seen at its best from the slow approach of the no. 82 water-bus) to Palladio's designs and the current excellent state of repair to the fact that it is owned by the Fondazione Giorgio Cini. You will land near the church's parvis-square *(open 9-12.30/14.30-16.30; Summer 18.30)*, and the Palladian façade is cadenced in three parts by composite columns. The interior is a splendid reinterpretation of a Latin cross plan with transept, enhanced by canvases by Tintoretto *(note the Last Supper)* **(6)**, a 16th-century wooden choir and by a St George and the Dragon by Vittore Carpac-

cio, dated 1516. Palladio also designed the cloister that is the heart of the monastery *(by appointment, tel. 0415289900)*, and whose interior is embellished by 17th-century architectural gems by Baldassarre Longhena that include a dual-ramp staircase and a library.

(1)

furnishings in the late 18th century, and then the second *piano nobile:* here tourists visit mainly the rooms of the Anticollegio (rebuilt by Palladio, with 16th-century works by Paolo Veronese, Tintoretto and Jacopo Bassano) and the Collegio (designed by Palladio and again with frescoes by Veronese and Tintoretto). The most important elements, however, are the **Maggior Consiglio room** (used by the magistrature, the most important in La Serenissima, and all nobles registered in the "Libro d'Oro" were members), decorated with a sequence of canvases by Palma the Younger, Tintoretto (*Vision of Paradise,* on the dais wall) and Paolo Veronese (*Apotheosis,* ceiling); and the **Bridge of Sighs (1)**, built in the 17th century across the rear canal to connect the building to the new prisons.

12. Riva degli Schiavoni

"Schiavoni" was the name given to the merchants who came from what is now Dalmatia, which was under Venetian dominion for centuries, and one of Venice's historic trading places is named after them **(2)**. In fact, where gondolas, water-buses and other boats now huddle – and where one of the city's loveliest strolls begins – was the landing point for vessels packed with goods, up until the fall of the Republic.

13. San Zaccaria

Mon.-Sat. 10-12 and 16-18; Sun. 16-18

To shrug off the noisy crowds on the Riva and slip into a concealed nook of Venice, simply enter the Sottoportego San Zaccaria and on the right you will see the façade of the San Zaccaria church, built in 1440-90. It is dominated by Renaissance lines (Istrian stone) overlaying the Gothic (multi-coloured marble), whereas the interior features the contrary (note the polygonal apse). On the left wall, Giovanni Bellini's magnificent altarpiece (1505), set against the backdrop of frescoes by Andrea del Castagno and Francesco da Faenza (1442), not to mention three Gothic polyptychs by Antonio Vivarini and Giovanni d'Alemagna (1443) in the San Tarasio chapel.

14. San Giovanni in Bragora

Mon.-Sat. 9-11/15.30-18.30

In 1678 Antonio Vivaldi **(3)**, the famous composer, was baptised in this church, also set back slightly north of Riva degli Schiavoni. Its Gothic outline dates back to rebuilding from 1475-79. The corpus of masterpieces inside the nave and two-aisle church dates back to the second half of this same century: Bartolomeo Vivarini painted the triptych on the right aisle, Alvise Vivarini created the *Risen Christ* next to the sacristy door; Cima da Conegliano painted the *Baptism of Jesus* on the high altar.

15. Arsenale

The galleys that sailed the eastern Mediterranean, intent on missions of peace and war, flying the flag of St Mark, were

(3)

(2)

built not far from San Giovanni in Bragora, in the vast Arsenale complex, said to have been operating as early as the 12th century and which continued to grow at least until the 1500s. The long, walled perimeter is reinforced by canals and broken on the land side by a portal considered to be the first Renaissance-style document in the city **(4)**. Water-bus no. 52 is the only means available for visiting the interior, still under restoration in the east part of the canal, but already in partial use for Biennale exhibits.

16. Museo Storico Navale

Mon.-Fri. 8.45-13.30, Sat. 8.45-13

The magnificence of the Arsenal is brought to life in the Naval History Museum **(5)**, where the rio (side canal) of the same name opens into the Lagoon, set up in an indoor section of an old warehouse (here you will find a model

of the last **Bucintoro**, the Doge's parade vessel) and in an outdoor section, opening onto the canal.

17. Giardini Pubblici

Although the period of French domination was short-lived, it was important for Venice from a city-planning aspect. In a city that virtually lacked any green spaces, the urban furnishing ideals inspired by the Revolution brought the installation of Public Gardens, which are Venice's biggest area of nature and extend almost to the end of the San Marco canal. The original neo-classical layout has survived along Via Garibaldi, whilst the southernmost section in part resembles a romantic English garden, but above all is linked to the international art Biennale, invented in 1895 by the mayor of the time, Riccardo Selvatico and which became one of the 20th century's greatest painting, sculpture and graphics events; in point of fact, from the early 1900s to 1964, the park was installed with a series of pavilions designed by the cream of contemporary architects.

(5)

(4)

18. San Pietro di Castello

Mon.-Sat. 10-17; Sun. 13-17

Before St Mark's basilica became the cathedral of Venice (1807), this role was played by the church of San Pietro di Castello, built on the island of Castello, which gave the sestiere (or district) its name in the 9th century, and refurbished several times **(6)**.

The last intervention was undertaken at the turn of 16th and 17th century, to designs by Palladio, which explains the lines of the façade and the equilibrium between the nave and two aisles, with the cupola near the crossing; if the Vendramin chapel is an essay in Baroque architecture by Longhena, the Lando (1425) chapel is the only surviving testimony of the previous place of worship. A titbit: the nearby late 1400s belfry is the only one in the city totally finished in Istrian stone.

(6)

FROM MERCERIE TO

*G*reat monuments that are visited by tourists from every corner of the world, but also more secluded zones, neglected by day-trippers, are characteristic of the west area of Venice, embraced by the Castello district, which in the past was colonized by several religious

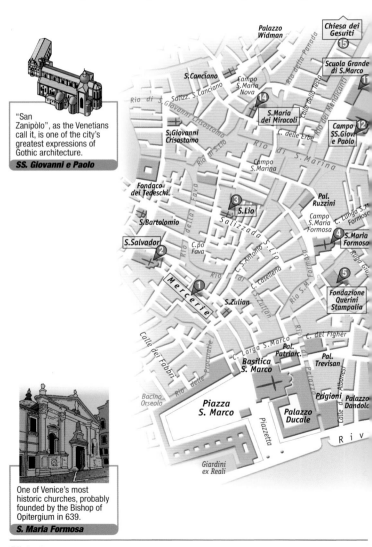

"San Zanipòlo", as the Venetians call it, is one of the city's greatest expressions of Gothic architecture.
SS. Giovanni e Paolo

One of Venice's most historic churches, probably founded by the Bishop of Opitergium in 639.
S. Maria Formosa

FONDAMENTA NUOVE

orders (Franciscans, Dominicans and Jesuits) and foreign communities
(Greeks, Slavs). Part of La Serenissima's charm emerges precisely from
observation of the urban fabric crossed in the long stroll between
one pause and the next.

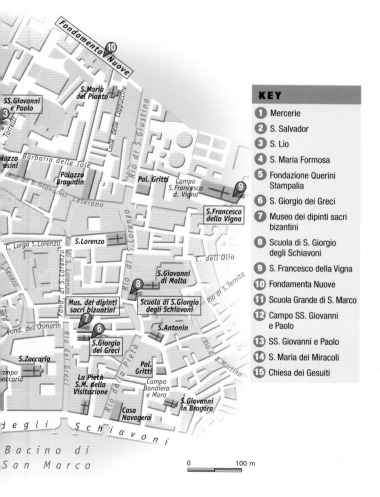

KEY

1. Mercerie
2. S. Salvador
3. S. Lio
4. S. Maria Formosa
5. Fondazione Querini Stampalia
6. S. Giorgio dei Greci
7. Museo dei dipinti sacri bizantini
8. Scuola di S. Giorgio degli Schiavoni
9. S. Francesco della Vigna
10. Fondamenta Nuove
11. Scuola Grande di S. Marco
12. Campo SS. Giovanni e Paolo
13. SS. Giovanni e Paolo
14. S. Maria dei Miracoli
15. Chiesa dei Gesuiti

1. Le Mercerie

Le Mercerie was the first Venetian road to be paved, as early as the 13th century, suggesting the importance of the historic route between Piazza San Marco (beginning beyond the great arch that opens underneath the clock tower) and the Rialto area. The name itself recalls that its vocation was strictly commercial, confirmed even today by the shops – now many of them are high fashion boutiques – that open onto it.

2. San Salvador

Mon.-Sat. 9-12/15-18; Sun. 15-18; Summer 16-18

Tradition has the church founded even as early as the 7th century, but the building seen at the end of Le Mercerie is a 1600s façade and the interior is also completely Renaissance, with a nave and two aisles, but on a Greek cross plan, so

(1)

What's a bòvolo?

In Venetian dialect a "bòvolo" is a winding staircase installed outside of Gothic houses **(2)**. One of La Serenissima's buildings is so famous for this structure that the word was ab-

(2)

sorbed by the name: Palazzo Contarini del Bòvolo, concealed in the dense network of alleys south-west of San Salvador church: the staircase in question is in the inner courtyard and resembles a round tower whose exterior is enhanced by small arches on columns.

much later (16th century) than the supposed laying of the first stone. There is also a mysterious notion that in 1177 this was the meeting place for Pope Alexander III and his archenemy Frederic Barbarossa, before Titian had painted the *Annunciation* **(1)** (1566) on the third right-hand altar, signed with his motto "fecit fecit".

3. San Lio

The church, nestling hidden to the east of San Salvador, is similar in date to it. It was built not long after (9th century) and its overall appearance is 17th century, like San Salvador. The exterior is quite bland and unassuming, but redeemed by the sequence of ceiling frescoes by Giandomenico Tiepolo (1783) and by a canvas by Titian on the first left-hand altar.

4. Santa Maria Formosa

Mon.-Sat. 10-17; Sun. 13-17

The *calle* that bears off to the left at the bottom of Salizzada San Lio crosses a rio and ends in front of the church façade **(3)**, said to have been founded by the Bishop of Opitergium in 639 (so it would be one of the oldest in Venice) after the apparition of a lovely Madonna (hence the name "formosa").

The main façade does

(

not support this date as it was erected in the 17th century and neither does the façade in the side canal, which dates back to the previous century. Useless to seek any confirmation in the interior as it was refurbished at the end of the 15th century by Mauro Codussi in Renaissance style, with a hint of Byzantine; Bartolomeo Vivarini's Venetian school triptych in the third chapel to the right is an essay of the same period.

5. Fondazione Querini Stampalia
Tue.-Thu. and Sun. 10-18; Fri.-Sat. 10-22

Another refined example of Venetian collecting is the corpus of works, pride of the Foundation, established just after 1850 by the last member of the Querini Stampalia family, in the 16th-century ancestral home **(4)**. Nowadays there are three reasons for visiting the building, very near to Campo Santa Maria Formosa. Those wishing to consult historic texts go to the library, which also has precious maps. Enthusiasts of 19th-20th-century Venetian painting visit the picture gallery, attracted by the *Presentation of Jesus in the Temple*, by Giovanni Bellini, by genre paintings by the 18th-century Pietro Longhi, by the portrait of a member of the Dolfin family by Giambattista Tiepolo and

(4)

by a drawing by Antonio Canova.
Lastly, those who enjoy a drink in an atmosphere steeped in culture, sit at the tables of the **Florian Artecaffè.**

6. San Giorgio dei Greci
Wed.-Mon. 9-13/15-16.30; Sun. 9-13

An ephemeral link connects the Querini Stampalia Foundation with the nearby church of San Giorgio dei Greci **(5)**.
Part of the surname of that

family derives from the fact that for many years the Querini owned the island of Stampalia, in Greece. The community that undertook the building of the church of San Giorgio dei Greci came precisely from there and even today an orthodox mass is held, with abundant use of incense. Although it dates back to 1539-62, the place of worship is Renaissance even in the façade, which echoes Sansovino's models; the cupola and oddly tilted belfry are also 16th century. Although the exterior is "western" in form, the interior is typical of orthodox churches, where the iconostasis is still used to separate the nave from the presbytery; the gold backdrop panels that embellish it are Late Byzantine.

(5)

7. Museo dei dipinti sacri Bizantini
9-17

(1)

The sing-song cadences of the Greek language echo in all the buildings around the church, occupied by institutions connected to that community. The Scuola di San Nicolò dei Greci, 1600s architecture by Baldassarre Longhena, houses the museum of Byzantine religious art, with a series of icons **(1)** that illustrate local Greek production with two themes: the Virgin Mary and Jesus.

8. Scuola di San Giorgio degli Schiavoni
Tue.-Sat. 10-12.30 and 15-18; Sun. 10-12.30; Summer 9.30-12.30/15.30-18.30

The Scuola di San Giorgio is attributable to the foreign order of the "Schiavoni" from Dalmatia and was commissioned in 1451 but with the façade in Istrian stone added in the 16th century, inspired by Sansovino's models. The French "fury" for confiscation in the late 18th century did not dare to attempt a transfer to the banks of the Seine of the cycles that Vittore Carpaccio painted in 1501-11, dedicating them to the community's patron saints (St George, but also St Trifon, patron of Catharum). The story begins on the left-hand wall with the marvellous *St George killing the dragon* **(2)**, followed by the *Saint's Triumph*; the same saint returns on the back wall as he baptises the King and Queen of Libya, accompanied, beyond the altar, by the *Miracle of St Trifon*; on the right-hand wall two episodes of the *Gospels* precede a third figure linked to Dalmatia (*St Jerome with the tamed lion* and *the Saint's funeral rites*) and the Vision of St Augustine, famous for the meticulous depiction of a 15th century study (religious tradition attributes it with a resemblance to Cardinal Bessarione).

The "scuole"

The expression identifies one of Venice's most typical monuments and derives from the Latin scholae, initially indicating where craftsmen's guilds met, formed to offer assistance. Eventually the word was applied to the entire association. More than 200 are documented in the city, both large and small, dedicated to the patron saint of each skill; initially there was just a small altar but as time passed they became proper buildings, which the confraternities ordered to be decorated to celebrate their wealth and importance, commissioning great artists, like Carpaccio for the Schiavoni and Tintoretto for San Rocco **(6)**.

(6)

9. San Francesco della Vigna
8.30-12.30 and 15-19

The tall belfry, reminiscent of St Mark's, points in the direction of the church that the Franciscans decided to build in

(2)

(3)

1300, in a vineyard that they owned at that time **(3)**. Today, however, everything about the place of worship echoes the reconstruction "sponsored" by the Doges Gritti and Grimani, and entrusted in 1534-82 to Sansovino and then to Palladio. The latter con-

(4)

structed the façade, structured in two orders and with a double gable, whereas the interior is clearly influenced by Sansovino's ideas of how a place of worship should be: classical, with the plain architectural expression typical of Tuscany. Canvases and sculptures make this a sort of small museum, with the many masterpieces in the side chapels dedicated to the great families of Venice: impossible not to linger

before the Antonio Vivarini triptych on the counterfaçade, with *Madonna and Child and Angels*, by Antonio da Negroponte (the only sure work by him, signed and dated 1470) on the first altar in the right-hand transept, to the Andrea and Triadano Gritti funeral monuments in the presbytery (mid-16th century and attributed to Sansovino), to the marble sculptures by Pietro Lombardo (1495-1510) in the Giustiniani chapel (left-hand transept), and a panel by Giovanni Bellini in the Cappella Santa **(4)**.

10. Fondamenta Nuove

If Riva degli Schiavoni is the best standpoint for gazing on the island of San Giorgio Maggiore and Le Zattere for facing Giudecca, the Fondamenta Nuove offer wonderful views of the northern part of the Lagoon, with the island of San Michele slipping in just in front of Murano, whilst on a clear day it may be possible to glimpse Burano and Torcello in the distance. This long perspective was created in the mid-16th century and the first section coasts a series of religious buildings that were linked in the 19th century to open the city hospital.

11. Scuola Grande di San Marco

Mon.-Fri. 8.30-14

The long prospect of the hospital structures facing Rio dei Mendicanti, almost at the opening of the Fondamenta of the same name in Campo SS. Giovanni and Paolo, is formed by the façade of the Scuola **(5)** founded by the Mendicant confraternity but rebuilt following a

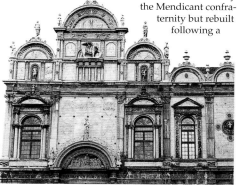

(5)

fire in the late 15th century and then extended in the following century, by Sansovino. The exterior is hallmarked by its multi-coloured elegance and harmonic proportions, with a particularly interesting asymmetrical prospect facing the campo (the left corresponds to the actual Scuola, whereas the right belonged to the annexed accommodation): splendid, late 1400s sculptures blend in with the circular fronton coping and faux architectural perspectives. The sensation of standing before one of the bulwarks of Venetian Renaissance architecture is confirmed by the interior, with canvases by Palma the Younger and Domenico Tintoretto.

12. Campo SS. Giovanni and Paolo

As well as the traditional well-curb (16th century), the square is also installed with something that is quite rare in the city, a handsome **equestrian monument to Bartolomeo Colleoni (1)**, a condottiero of Bergamasque origins who was often a mercenary for

(1)

The graveyard of Venice

Plunged in the silence of the Lagoon, the island of San Michele, reached by the 41 and 42 water-buses from Fondamenta Nuove, has been used as La Serenissima's cemetery since the turn of the 19th century. This drastic "change in use" for a scrap of land consecrated to St Michael the Archangel in the 10th century, then location of a Camaldolese monastery in the early 13th century, was ordered by the occupying French who applied the Saint-Cloud edict to the Lagoon, abolishing the unhygienic practice of burying the dead in churches. The church of San Michele in Isola (*7.30-16; Summer 7.30-18*) serves to recall the island's ancient vocation as a spiritual retreat, and the water-bus docks before a Renaissance façade in Istrian stone, built in the 15th century by Mauro Codussi, but with a 16th-century addition of the Emiliani chapel, to the left of the prospect; the interior is carpeted with tombstones (the grave of Paolo Sarpi amongst others). Illustrious Venetians rest in peace in the nearby cemetery.

La Serenissima: the opus is by Andrea Verrocchio (1481-88) and should have been located in front of St Mark's basilica (promised by the Doges despite knowing the law forbade it), but an audacious pun had it installed in front of the Scuola Grande di San Marco.

13. SS. Giovanni and Paolo

Mon.-Sat. 9.30-18; Sun. 13-18

"San Zanipòlo" is the more familiar name of the SS. Giovanni and Paolo basilica, fundamentally important on La Serenissima's historical and cultural horizons since it is one of the greatest expressions of Gothic and where a doge's funeral would be officiated. It is the fruit of almost two hundred years of building efforts (1246-1430), has a streamlined façade whose central, tallest section, culminates in three soaring pinnacles and under the pitched roof is

(2)

embroidered with small vaulted arches; below, the arches hold the tombs of the Doges, as does the right side, and from there it is possible to observe marvellous Late Gothic polygonal apses **(2)**. The size of the interior **(3)** is worthy of one of the Dominator's greatest places of worship. The counterfaçade is dedicated to the Doges of the Mocenigo family (the most noteworthy is the monument to Pietro, dating back to 1476-81); the polyptych

(3)

of St Vincent Ferrer (1464 or thereabouts), on the second altar of the right aisle, is an early masterpiece by Giovanni Bellini, and the *Glory of St Dominic* (1725-27), in the San Domenico chapel, is one of the greatest works by Giovan Battista Piazzetta. The panels of the great Gothic window in the right transept celebrate the Dominican order who "sponsored" the building. Doge sepulchres are also installed in the neighbouring presbytery (the 15th-century monument to Andrea Vendramin is here), continuing down the left aisle nave, dominated by the monument to Pasquale Malipiero (thought to be the first in Renaissance style in the city) and another to Tommaso Mocenigo (by the Tuscans Pietro Lamberti and Giovanni di Martino).

14. Santa Maria dei Miracoli
Mon.-Sat. 10-17

The church is a pure Renaissance expression, another eloquent declaration of the style in the Lagoon, aligning the calle with the basilica. It features multicoloured marble and a façade of pure lines, structured in two orders outlined by pilaster strips, with a circular fronton lightened by rosettes, where the ornamental marble is accompanied by a wooden caisson ceiling dated 14th century and Niccolò di Pietro's *Madonna and Child*, to whom the church is dedicated.

15. Chiesa dei Gesuiti
10-12 and 16-18

You must cross a dense and still quite characteristic fabric of buildings to reach Fondamenta Nuove, near the church that in Venice is perhaps the most typical of the counter-reform architectural canons dictated by the Jesuit order **(4)**. In point of fact, it was the order founded by Ignatius of Loyola that in the 18th century rebuilt a place of worship that was already present in the previous century, seeking inspiration in the Gesù church in Rome, both for the two-order façade and the aisleless interior with side chapels. It has no equal in the city and here the white and green marble intarsia decoration weaves a tapestry effect; the white and gold stuccoes are a handsome complement, with a floor played out in black and white. Such a rich ornamentation might risk overshadowing Titian's canvas (1588) on the first altar in the left-hand nave.

(4)

FROM SAN MARCO

If the San Marco sestiere is bursting with visitors, even in its remotest nooks, so the Dorsoduro area is able to retain that emotion of strolling without meeting a living soul, despite the "heavyweight" presence

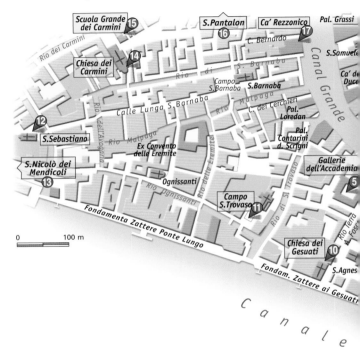

KEY

1. Campo S. Fantin
2. S. Maria del Giglio
3. S. Stefano
4. Ponte dell'Accademia
5. Gallerie dell'Accademia
6. Collezione Peggy Guggenheim
7. S. Maria della Salute
8. Punta della Dogana
9. Le Zattere
10. Chiesa dei Gesuati
11. Campo S. Trovaso
12. S. Sebastiano
13. S. Nicolò dei Mendicoli
14. Chiesa dei Carmini
15. Scuola Grande dei Carmini
16. S. Pantalon
17. Ca' Rezzonico

TO CA' REZZONICO

of frontline tourist destinations like the Accademia, La Salute and Ca' Rezzonico. You will encounter only Venetians and lovers of the so-called "minor", which offers magical surprises precisely in this part of the city.

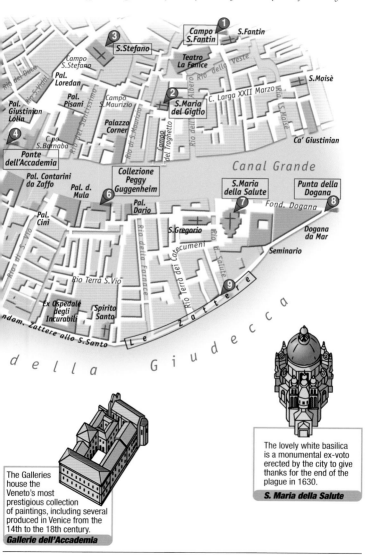

The Galleries house the Veneto's most prestigious collection of paintings, including several produced in Venice from the 14th to the 18th century.
Gallerie dell'Accademia

The lovely white basilica is a monumental ex-voto erected by the city to give thanks for the end of the plague in 1630.
S. Maria della Salute

1. Campo San Fantin

On 29 January 1996 **"La Fenice"**, the opera house that had been a prestigious location worldwide, was destroyed in a fire. The rebuilding was finally completed in late 2003, restoring the theatre to its historic splendour. The theatre can be visited accompanied by guides speaking various languages *(www.teatro-lafenice.it, tel. 0412424)*. There are also two significant Venetian monuments in this square: **the church of San Fantin** *(8-12 and 16-19)*, still immersed in mystery as to whether it is in part by Sansovino, from the 1500s, or 1500-1600s and by Lombardo; **the former Scuola di San Fantin** *(by appointment, tel. 0415224459)*, also 1500-1600s, and since 1812 home of the Ateneo Veneto, founded by Napoleon, with ceilings in the Great Hall (Aula Magna) decorated with canvases by Palma the Younger and the reading room by Tintoretto.

2. Santa Maria del Giglio

Mon.-Sat. 10-17

Santa Maria del Giglio, set on the main thoroughfare for the Accademia, has origins in the early Middle Ages (10th century), but any trace of this disappeared after the 17th century, when it was totally rebuilt **(1)**. The façade is mightily decorated with a sequence of statues whose objective is to celebrate those "sponsoring" the reconstruction. There are six *views of Italian and Dalmatian cities*, a masterpiece by Tintoretto (1552) set intriguingly on the façade, and equally intriguing are the *Evangelists* in the presbytery.

www.palazzograssi.it

In the era of the internet, the website *www.palazzograssi.it* is the quickest, least expensive way to acquire real-time information about the programme of events organized by the Grassi Foundation, as well as opening hours for Palazzo Grassi **(3)** exhibits. From the same website you can download information about the building, erected in the 18th century, not far from Campo Santo Stefano, with a mock-classical prospect looking out over the Grand Canal; its restoration was entrusted to Gae Aulenti.

(3)

(2)

3. Santo Stefano

Mon.-Sat. 10-17; Sun. 13-17

The Augustinians began this construction in Campo Santo Stefano **(2)** in 1294 but it was not completed until the 15th century. You would be well advised to catch a classical concert here as the Gothic interior is truly charming, with a wooden costola ceiling that produces good acoustics, but the numerous works of art will be a distraction from the music. It is worth returning to the church when there are no concerts scheduled, so you can visit the sacristy, with its

(1)

three Tintorettos and a wonderful Crucifixion by Paolo Veneziano (14th century).

4. Ponte dell'Accademia

In a chronological and historical sense, this is the second of the Grand Canal bridges and it is extremely busy as it is the gateway to Dorsoduro for anyone arriving from San Marco **(4).** Oddly enough, when it

(4)

was built in 1854 it was to be temporary but after the 1934 refurbishment it has acquired its own historical significance.

5. Gallerie dell'Accademia

Mon. 8.15-14;
Tue.-Sun. 8.15-19.15

The most prestigious collection of paintings in the Veneto Region – and one of Italy's greatest outright – is the "side effect" on one hand of the French regime's suppression of churches and places of worship, and on the other hand the creation of the Accade-

mia di Belle Arti (Academy of Fine Arts). The Galleries were established in 1807 and shortly after were opened to the public, occupying part of the Santa Maria della Carità complex, emerging from the 14th century and comprising the church of the same name (included in the museum itinerary) and the former monastery behind it, all now occupied by the Accademia.

The Venetian and Veneto works of art, dating from the 14th to the 18th century, are exhibited prevalently in chronological order, and many are shown in the historic context of the complex. For instance from the

ticket desk you will go up to the room used by the Santa Maria della Carità confraternity for its meetings: this explains the lovely gilt, 15th-century coffered ceiling, not to mention the polyptychs and panels with gold background that are the work of the so-called Veneto primitives (late 14th-early 15th century), as well as the processional cross of St Theodore, an example of Venetian goldsmith's craft of that era. The St Job altarpiece (1487c.), Giovanni Bellini's masterpiece and example of local production at the turn of the 15th-16th century, dominates the room originally set aside for Titian's *Assumption*, now in the Frari. The city's open-minded attitude to external influences is seen in the *St George* (1466-67) by Mantegna who was from Padua, *St Jerome and a Donor* (1450c.) by the Tuscan Piero della Francesca and the *Madonna of the Zodiac* (1455c.) by Cosmè Tura of Ferrara; Gothic lines were totally set aside for Renaissance trends in the *Madonna*

Museo Fortuny

(5)

Palazzo Fortuny, thus named after Mariano Fortuny y Madrazo, who purchased it in the early 20th century **(5)**, could be defined an artist's house. This Spanish painter and set-designer arranged his collections in this building, with its original 15th-century plan (in the courtyard you will see the outside, porticoed stairs), and created the Fortuny Museum *(now closed for restoration)*. The palazzo is slightly north east of Santo Stefano.

(1)

and Child with Saints, also by Bellini. This artist dominates the next room with one of his greatest productions (*Pietà* dated 1505) **(1)**, duelling with two masterpieces by Giorgione (the well-known *Tempest* and The *Old Woman*, 1508). The first half of the 16th century, artistically speaking, is monopolized by Titian (*St John the Baptist*, 1542; *Pietà*), Lorenzo Lotto (*Portrait of a Gentleman*), Palma the Younger (*Holy Conversation*, 1523-25), Paolo Veronese (*Supper at Levi's house*) and Tintoretto (large canvases for the Scuola Grande di San Marco). The greatest Italian names – and several of the most important from abroad – il-

(2)

lustrate taste from the 1650s through to the 18th century, the period of the *views* and *landscapes* signed by Francesco Guardi, Bernardo Bellotto and Canaletto **(2)**. There is then a leap back in time of 300 years, returning to the 15th century, with the *Miracles of the Holy Cross*, a sequence of large canvases painted for the Scuola Grande di San Giovanni Evangelista by Vittore Carpaccio (*Miracle of the Relic of the Cross at the Rialto Bridge*), Giovanni Mansueti, Gentile Bellini (*Miracle of the Cross fallen into the San Lorenzo Canal and the Procession in Piazza San Marco*), Benedetto Diana and Lazzaro Bastiani. Practically contemporaries of these are the large canvases of the *Life of St Ursula* that Carpaccio painted in 1490-96 for the Scuola di Sant'Orsola oratory, creating a masterpiece hallmarked by its secularity, both in the references to life at that time and for the use of what was clearly the Lagoon in the backgrounds. Post-1650 works are all housed in the former church of Santa Maria della Carità, with excellent examples like *Blessed Lorenzo Giustiniani* by Gentile Bellini and Paris Bordone's Presentation of the *Ring to the Doge*. The final room in the Gallery is also historic: the Albergo della Scuola room, with its Renaissance ceiling in blue and gold, enhanced by Titian's *Presentation of the Virgin* (1534-39; the only work in the muse-

(3)

um still in its original location) and a triptych by Antonio Vivarini and Giovanni d'Alemagna (1446).

6. Collezione Peggy Guggenheim
10-18

Alongside New York and Bilbao, Venice enjoys the privilege of hosting a branch of the extremely prestigious "Salomon R. Guggenheim Foundation", which owns the 20th century works of art collected by the millionaire Peggy Guggenheim. The Collection is in **Palazzo Venier dei Leoni (3)**, to the east of the Gallerie dell'Accademia, stretch-

(4)

ing towards La Salute and although only a limited number of works can be shown at any one time, they do document practically all 20th-century artistic currents, with Peggy Guggenheim's evident penchant for Surrealism and Jackson Pollock. The corpus embraces from Picasso's Cubism (*The Poet*, dated 1911, is the oldest work in the Collection) to abstracts by Piet Mondrian and the Italian Futurists Giacomo Balla and Giorgio De Chirico, closing with the Surrealists Salvador Dalí and Juan Miró.

7. Santa Maria della Salute
9-12 and 15.30-18

Every 21 November a bridge of boats is created across the Grand Canal to allow the procession in honour of the presentation of Our Lady to go from Piazza San Marco to the basilica of Santa Maria della Salute, the gigantic ex-voto com-

missioned by the city from Longhena to celebrate the end of the plague. It was begun in 1630 but it was completed in 1687, by which time the procession was in its sixth year, and by then its white, cupola-topped mole was an indelible mark on the Venice skyline. This is supported by a refined play of volumes that is best expressed from the interior, where the central area is cadenced by pillars and columns that hold the drum, and surrounded by a corridor serving chapels and the presbytery. The canvases are all a celebration of the Virgin, with the most important works in the sacristy: there are works by Titian both in the ceiling (1543) and on the altar (1512), whilst you will find Tintoretto's *Marriage of Cana*, and a 12th-century Byzantine *Madonna and Child* in the tabernacle **(4)**.

8. Punta della Dogana

The east front of the basilica parvis-square is closed by Dogana da Mar, a building shaped like a ship's prow, erected between the 15th and 19th centuries as a port for goods arriving by sea. The point of the construction, the actual "punta della Dogana", is characterised by a white arcade surmounted by a tower: above this, two bronze atlases with a golden globe that in turn holds a statue of *Fortune* that turns in the wind.

9. Le Zattere

Just around the point you glimpse Giudecca island, so Le Zattere immediately confirm their fame as one of the loveliest strolls in the city, reaching as far as the sea passenger terminal **(5)**. The name "Le Zattere" derives from the type of vessel that alternated with wherries to trans-

(5)

Giudecca Island

The stroll along Le Zattere **(1)** is accompanied by an island, just beyond a branch of the Lagoon, that has retained calm, relaxing atmospheres and pace, despite being a stone's throw from the city's heartbeat. That is why it is popular with connoisseurs, whereas most tourists just gaze from a distance at its most important monument: Palladio's Redentore church. Water-buses 41, 42 and 82 approach it slowly and leave you time to mull over the suggested origins of its name: some say it has to do with the Jews, others that in the past several parts of the island were given to citizens unjustly judged ("zudecare" in Venetian dialect). But also to observe the **Zitelle** complex, built at the end of the 16th century, perhaps designed by Palladio, to help young poor women (in fact the full name is Santa Maria della Presentazione). The later **Redentore church** *(Mon.-Sat. 10-17)* is certainly by that architect. This church is the destination of another bridge of boats that forms in July to cross the Giudecca canal for the feast of the Redeemer; commissioned by the Venetian Senate to call upon the Redeemer to free the city of a plague epidemic that broke out in 1575, the church was not finished until 1592, even though the procession had begun as early as 1576, when the epidemic miraculously ended a few months after the laying of the first stone. Its façade has typical Palladian forms, set high on a staircase and layered into three orders by half columns and pilaster strips to support the tympanum. Some explain the interior's complex layout as being required by the annual procession, which is also linked to the unifying theme pervading the sculptures and paintings: redemption through Christ's crucifixion, depicted by artists that include Palma the Younger and Tintoretto. The island's oldest place of worship is the **Sant'Eufemia church,** dated 9th century but remodelled so many times that only the interior has retained its original form and in it you will find a triptych by Bartolomeo Vivarini (1480). Late in the 19th century the island was reconverted for production purposes and the **ex-Mulino Stucky (2)** was erected as an impressive neo-Gothic complex inspired by Northern Europe, it then fell into disuse after WWII and, after a long period of abandon, was partially destroyed by fire during its recovery for the service industry.

(1)

(2)

port the goods stored here, whereas the names of the individual sections refer to the main points around it. First the Saloni, salt warehouses now partially recovered as an exhibition space; then the Renaissance-style Spirito Santo church.

10. Chiesa dei Gesuati

Mon.-Sat. 10-17

The observant visitor will notice a resemblance between this façade and that of the Redentore church opposite **(3)**. In point of fact, this place of worship, which ceased to belong to the Jesuate congregation in 17th century, was rebuilt in the 18th with a Late Baroque form with some elements typical of Palladian expression, like the overriding schema of the actual prospect. A refined play of light and colour makes the interior quite

(3)

charming, where the theme of the Rosary (in fact the church is dedicated to Our Lady of the Rosary) was celebrated in the ceiling by Giambattista Tiepolo, who is also the author of the canvas near the first altar to the right, and of the apse frescoes.

11. Campo San Trovaso

Right after Ponte Lungo which marks the start of the last section of Le Zattere, San Trovaso side ca-

(4)

nal laps the left of a square that is rendered quite unique by one of Venice's last surviving *boat-houses*: it is the dark wood and brick structure preceded by the ramp down to the water, where gondolas were repaired from the 17th century. The church of San Trovaso **(4)** is also located here *(Mon.-Sat. 10-17)*, founded in the Middle Ages but later rebuilt in the late 16th century, which surprisingly houses a group of works by Tintoretto.

12. San Sebastiano
Mon.-Sat. 10-17

You will have to really search out this 16th-century church **(5),** off the mass tourist beaten track (actually it is near the sea passenger terminal at the end of Le Zattere). Despite its being a little distance from the centre, it is certainly worth visiting if you are interested in 16th-century Renaissance painting: the cycles of works produced in various stages by Paolo Veronese can be seen inside. This pictorial venture began in 1555 in the sacristy, which is the location of the city's first Veronese opus; the following year he continued working in the nave, where you will see the marvellous *Esther taken before Ahasuerus, Coronation of Esther and Triumph*

(5)

of Mordecai; then (1560) along the nave; and last (1561) the presbytery.

13. San Nicolò dei Mendicoli
Mon.-Sat. 10-12 and 16-18

Certainly you will not be disappointed by a stroll through the area west of San Sebastiano to reach San Nicolò dei Mendicoli **(6)** because you will encounter an aspect of La Serenissima that most

(6)

people are unfamiliar with, and precisely because this area conceals one of the few surviving places of worship in Venetian-Byzantine style. The church of San Nicolò dei Mendicoli still has its 13th-century façade with a porch that served as shelter to beggars (in Venetian: "mendicoli") and a slightly older belfry.

(2)

14. Chiesa dei Carmini

Mon.-Sat. 7.30-12.30/14.30-17.30

Of the many confraternities present in the city, that of the Carmelites **(1)**, dedicated to our Lady of Mount Carmel, was one of the most powerful and prestigious, that to be elected a member was almost a status symbol. From San Nicolò dei Mendicoli, the street that coasts the rio towards north east, on the left enters a square, location of the congregation's church, whose Gothic and Renaissance elements document the lengthy construction time

(late 13th to early 16th century). The interior, however, is pure Gothic, with a nave and two aisles, the nave extending into the polygonal apse, whereas the partially gilt wooden decoration is 17th-century; splendid *Adoration of the Shepherds* by Cima da Conegliano dated 1509 (second altar in the left-hand nave) and Francesco di Giorgio Martini's bronze relief *Deposition* (1474) in the chapel to the right of the apse.

15. Scuola Grande dei Carmini

Summer 9-18; Winter 10-17

The power of the confraternity is also expressed by the annexed Scuola Grande, which was so prestigious that despite its suppression by Napoleon, achieved reintegration to its premises and patrimony as soon as the Austrians became rulers of Venice. The building is still arranged on two floors, with the upper storey housing nine canvases in the ceiling by Giambattista Tiepolo, dated 1739-44.

16. San Pantalon

Mon.-Sat. 15-18

La Serenissima has so many exquisite churches that some may unjustly fade into the background **(2)**. One such is located behind Campo Santa Margherita, with a decidedly anonymous façade but with a Baroque interior embellished with forty perspective-effect canvases and *Coronation of the Virgin* (1444) by Giovanni d'Alemagna and Antonio Vivarini in the chapel to the left of the main area.

17. Ca' Rezzonico

Apr.-Oct., Wed.-Mon. 10-18; Nov.-Tue., Wed.-Mon. 10-17

If you ask any of the many students heading for nearby Ca' Foscari University, you will have no trouble finding the right direction for what was one of Longhena's last enterprises, commissioned by the Bon family in 1649. Its current name refers to the family that bought the building in 1750 and then finished it. The ground-floor en-

(1)

trance, almost at the end of Rio San Barnaba, comprises an atrium that continues in the direction of the Grand Canal with the traditional sequence of an atrium with porch, a second hallway and an entrance porch on the façade; the latter faces out onto the city's main waterway and is set on a ground floor in masonry (where the portico opens), and has two *piano nobile* floors cadenced, respectively, by columns and pillars **(3).** The building is occupied by three important institutions. The Settecento Veneziano or **Venetian 1700s Museum** enjoys the palazzo's most typical rooms, and relates the last one hundred years of the Dominator's rule, with furniture, paintings and decorations. A monumental staircase takes to the first floor and the ballroom, whose furnishings are just a hint of what you will find in the subsequent rooms, often hallmarked by interventions by Giambattista Tiepolo (he frescoed the ceiling in the throne room **(4)** and his is the canvas in the ceiling of the room dedicated to him). The frescoes that Giandomenico Tiepolo painted in the late 18th century in Zianigo villa have been reassembled in several of the second floor

(4)

rooms; the Lacche Verdi room has splendid ceiling frescoes by Francesco Guardi, whilst genre paintings typical of that period by Pietro

(5)

Longhi and also by Guardi, enhance the Longhi **(5)** rooms and the Parlatorio. In the loft there is a **picture gallery** named after Egidio Martini who donated the canvases, mainly of the Venetian school and dated 15th-19th century. The **Ferruccio Mestrovic Collection** is a limited but refined example of a private collection.

(3)

37

SAN POLO, SANTA CROCE

*T*his is certainly a lengthy itinerary and possibly quite tiring if
you are not used to walking. Nevertheless, it is quite astonishing
for the sequence of exceptional monuments (in this part of the city

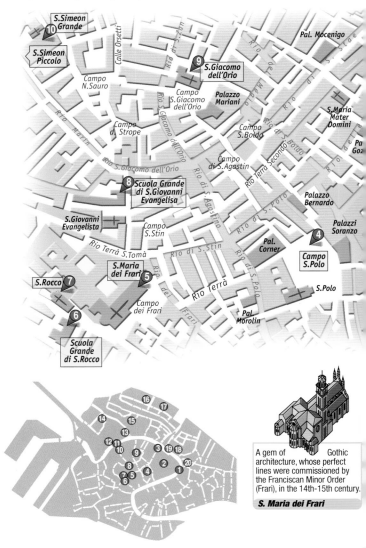

A gem of   Gothic
architecture, whose perfect
lines were commissioned by
the Franciscan Minor Order
(Frari), in the 14th-15th century.

S. Maria dei Frari

AND CANNAREGIO

you will meet Frari, Scuola Grande di San Rocco and Ca' d'Oro). From another perspective it is also quite amazing since tourist destinations of great appeal cohabit with a Venice that tourists barely know.

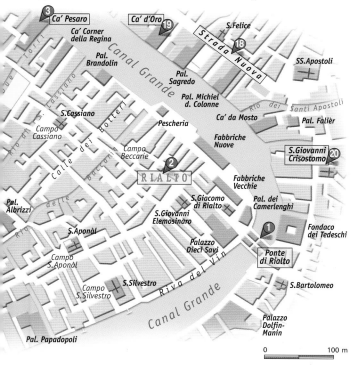

KEY

1. Ponte di Rialto
2. Rialto
3. Ca' Pesaro
4. Campo S. Polo
5. S. Maria dei Frari
6. Scuola Grande di S. Rocco
7. S. Rocco
8. Scuola Grande di S. Giovanni Evangelista
9. S. Giacomo dell'Orio
10. S. Simeon Grande e S. Simeon Piccolo
11. Ponte degli Scalzi
12. Chiesa degli Scalzi
13. Palazzo Labia
14. S. Giobbe
15. Il Ghetto
16. S. Alvise
17. Madonna dell'Orto
18. Strada Nuova
19. Ca' d'Oro
20. S. Crisostomo

(2)

1. Ponte di Rialto

Carpaccio's large canvas of the *Miracles of the Holy Cross*, now in the Gallerie dell'Accademia, depicts what was the only way of crossing the Grand Canal in the 15th century: a wooden bridge with a mobile central section **(1)**. In 1264 it had replaced the pontoons that "joined" the two banks, but it was short-lived: in the late 16th century it was actually replaced by today's single arch, which is split into three paths by rows of shops all meeting at

(1)

the apex of the arch **(2)**. The south of the passage looks left, at one of the historic locations of Venetian trade: the Ferro and Carbon banks, with rows of Medieval buildings (12th-13th century) of Venetian Byzantine forms. The north side of the bridge, to the right, has Fondaco dei Tedeschi, documented as early as the 13th century, but rebuilt in the 16th and with an exterior frescoed by Giorgione and Titian (these masterpieces are now in the Ca' d'Oro and in the Gallerie dell'Accademia), and to the left the Rialto district.

2. Rialto

This has always been the trading centre of La Serenissima, located where the Grand Canal sketches out a loop; at least since the 11th century, since the area had taller banks (the name Rialto means "high bank", from the Latin *rivoaltus*) and therefore enjoyed more protection from the waters. Inevitably the goods and their trade attracted businesses to the site and with the passing of time areas spe-

cialized, with individual products and activities concentrating in specific streets (this tradition survives only in the names of the streets, although the market lives on). What meets the eye at the peak of the bridge is an area that is in prevalence 16th century, the result of rebuilding subsequent to the 1514 fire and in part designed by Sansovino. Over the bridge, two structures

(3)

face one another: Palazzo dei Dieci Savi (left, home to the fiscal authorities) and Palazzo dei Camerlenghi (right, home to the finance authorities), both 16th century. Behind the latter you will find the small square and church of San Giacometto (12th century), which survived the blaze and is a worthy example of Venetian-Byzantine architecture (in the portico there are columns with Gothic capitals supporting an architrave still in wood); opposite you will see the Rialto hunchback **(3)**, a crouching figure holding the "colonna del Bando" from which public laws and notices were announced. On the right of San Giacometto, a vaulted passageway connects Fabbriche Vecchie (16th century) with contemporary Fabbriche Nuove, whilst the square behind, a mass of colour provided by the daily market, is closed by the neo-Gothic Pescheria.

3. Ca' Pesaro

Tues.-Sun. 10-17; Summer. 10-18

Baldassarre Longhena's genius as an architectural "great" of Venetian Baroque is confirmed by the building that houses the **Galleria d'Arte Moderna** (Gallery of Modern Art) and **Museo d'Arte Orientale** (Museum of Oriental Art) **(4)**. The Pesaro family commissioned Longhena to restructure three buildings of recent purchase:

the operations began in 1628, involving both the landward façade and the prospect looking out onto the Grand Canal, comprising a socle decorated with promotes of lions and monsters, and a dogtooth moulding base with portals surmounted by mascarons. The two upper storeys, with exquisite parapets, were completed early in the 18th century. The interior comprises a traditional court-entrance hall and since 1897 has housed the Gallery of Modern Art, intended to exhibit the works for the early Biennales and then enhanced to the point that it became one of the most important in Italy: all 20th-century currents are documented here, with artists like Giovanni Fattori, Umberto Boccioni, Giorgio De Chirico, Chagall, Gustave Klimt **(5)**, Paul Klee. The Museum

(5)

of Oriental Art focuses on the Edo period of Japanese art (1614-1868), created from the collections of Enrico of Bourbon, and some of these pieces are true rarities.

4. Campo San Polo

Excluding Piazza San Marco, this is Venice's biggest public space, stretching from southwest of Ca' Pesaro to Campo San Polo, whose sheer size made it a theatre for great religious and secular public events in bygone times, including bull hunts. It takes its name from the church of San Polo *(Mon.-Sat. 10-17)*, dedicated as early as the 9th century to the Apostle Paul (Polo is the dialect form of the name), but now with a neo-Classical exterior and 15th-century interior; its decoration was en-

(4)

trusted to three big names of Venetian painting bridging the 16th to the 18th century: Tintoretto (counter-façade and first altar on the right), Palma the Younger (presbytery) and Giambattista Tiepolo (second altar on the left and Crocifisso oratory).

(2)

5. Santa Maria dei Frari

Mon.-Sat. 10-17

Simply follow the flow of tourists going from San Polo to the basilica of Santa Maria Gloriosa dei Frari, which competes with San Zanipòlo as the crowning glory of Gothic architecture in La Serenissima **(1)**. The Franciscan Minors, known as the "Frari", who financed its construction in the 14th-15th century created a place of worship whose exterior betrays the austere forms of early Gothic, as well as subsequent,

more mature phases: it has a splendid pitched-roof façade, streamlined in the upper part by pilaster strips that form pinnacled arcades in the central section.

The interior **(2)** is pure Gothic, a nave and two aisles cadenced by pillars that support ogive arches, and cross-vaulting supported by wooden tie-rods.

(1)

The church has countless masterpieces: beginning with the Gothic-Renaissance choir that has occupied the centre of the basilica since 1475 and comprises more than 100 carved seats. That this place of worship is a sort of museum is confirmed by the Late Gothic monument to *Blessed Pacifico*, produced by the Tuscans Nanni di Bartolo and Michele da Firenze (1437; left transept arm), the marble tabernacle with the *Blood of Christ relic* (15th century) and the Giovanni Bellini triptych (1488) in the sacristy, the Bartolomeo Vivarini polyptych (1482; first right-hand apse chapel), the statue by Donatello (1450; third right-hand apse chapel), Titian's marvellous altarpiece of *Our Lady of the Assumption* (1516-18; high altar), the monument to Doge Niccolò Tron (1476; left presbytery wall) and the magnificent *Ca' Pesaro Madonna*, again by Titian (second altar in the left aisle).

6. Scuola Grande di San Rocco

Easter-Oct. 9-17.30; Nov.-Easter 10-16

Right behind the Frari you will find another one of Venice's "pièces de résistance". This is because the confraternity, perhaps the most important in the city, commissioned Tintoretto to decorate the building, constructed in 1515-24 in Renaissance forms and with a refined ornamental decoration (note the marble intarsia). From 1564 to 1587 the painter created one of his greatest masterpieces here, and one of the milestones of Mannerist art **(3)**. The interior has two floors: the ground floor salon houses what was actually Tintoretto's last work, to which he dedicated the period 1583-87, with an outstanding *Annunciation* **(4)**, *Flight from Egypt, Magdalene and St Maria Egiziaca*. The 16th-century stairway has two ramps that merge on the first floor: here you will

(4)

find the great salon decorated in 1576-81 with episodes from the *Old Testament* (ceiling) and *New Testament* (walls), and the Sala dell'Albergo, the first to be completed (1564-66), where the onlooker's eye is drawn to the *Crucifixion*, one of the rare works where Tintoretto leaves a signature and a date (1565).

7. San Rocco

8-12.30-15-17; Winter 8-12.30, Sat.-Sun. also 14-16

Tintoretto also worked on the confraternity

church, which closes the small square with a 1700s façade that conceals a late 15th-early 16th-century place of worship. The painter's corpus can be seen on the counter-façade, along the right-hand wall and in the presbytery.

8. Scuola Grande di San Giovanni Evangelista

By booking tel. 041718234

Before entering the Scuola, it is worth lingering to observe the unique structure of the square where it stands, which is reached from the San Rocco area by coasting the back of the old Frari complex: a marble structure, opening into gabled windows in the lower section and with a gabled portal surmounted by eagles that creates two separate spaces; the interior is the entrance to the building, begun in the mid-14th century but not completed until the 18th. The long period of construction is easily identified inside, with its 14th

(3)

century ground-floor salon (note the capitals), renaissance stairway and 18th-century upper salon, with the ceiling decorated with canvases on the theme of the *Apocalypse* (one by Giandomenico Tiepolo) and *Lives of the Saints* on the walls (in part by Domenico Tintoretto).

9. S. Giacomo dell'Orio
Mon.-Sat. 10-17

Rio San Giacomo dell'Orio, which runs north of the school, suggests the next destination, just beyond it. In the centre of this tree-lined, unusual for Venice, square **(1)**, there is a church with a surviving original 10th-century façade, although it was rebuilt in the 13th century and refurbished several times in the 16th-17th centuries. The nave and two-aisle interior, with the holy water font (13th century), retain their historic appearance; the chalice-shaped pulpit (15th-16th century) stands near a Ravenna-style column of the 6th century, with a Paolo

Veneziano (14th century) Crucifixion ceiling panel, but the real masterpiece is Lorenzo Lotto's *Madonna and Child* with Saints (1546; presbytery).

10. San Simeon Grande and San Simeon Piccolo
8.30-12 and 17-19

A duel played out on the size of the two places of worship, which are actually dedicated respectively to St Simeon the Prophet and Saints Simeon and Jude **(2)**. The former, San Simeon Grande, can be found slightly north-west of Campo San Giacomo dell'Orio and is thus known because it is slightly bigger than the other; it was rebuilt in the 18th century, and its Byzantine origins are documented only by the internal column capitals. The church of San

(2)

Simeon Piccolo looks out over the Grand Canal, precisely opposite the railway station and with the larger church shares a historic foundation and full 18th century reconstruction, but has a totally different plan, since this is a circular construction, decorated with a Corinthian pronaos with a bas relief in the tympanum.

The Ottoman seat of trade

La Serenissima applied quite buccaneer politics when dealing with the Turks: for centuries the city fought them to defend its Eastern Mediterranean possessions, but had no scruples in trading with them. The Turkish bastion was Fondaco dei Turchi **(5)**, an example of Venetian-Byzantine construction dated 12th-13th century; near Campo San Giacomo dell'Orio, looking out towards the Grand Canal, the prospect lightened in the central section by a portico and an arcade surmounted by crenellations and hugged by two towers; the interior houses the Natural History Museum (*Tues.-Fri. 9-13, Sat.-Sun. 10-16*)), which has some of the fossils discovered at Borca, in Veronese Lessinia.

(5)

(1)

11. Ponte degli Scalzi

Shortly after it became possible to reach Venice by train, a bridge had to be built between the two banks of the Grand Canal near the railway station. In 1858 an iron bridge was built and in 1934 this was replaced by the single-arch bridge that towers a full seven metres above the water surface.

12. Chiesa degli Scalzi

Mon.-Sat. 7-11.45 & 16-18.45; Sun. 7.45-12.30 & 16-19

Precisely because of its height, the bridge is a singular observation point for the church that the Barefoot Carmelites commissioned from Baldassarre Longhena in 1654, in honour of St Mary of Nazareth, which the architect finished in 1705, except for the façade. Behind the façade, structured in two orders with coupled columns, the interior refers to Roman models with multicoloured marble decoration and gildings, as well as the use of sculptures.

13. Palazzo Labia

Temporarily closed
tel. 041781268

To the right of the church, RAI's Veneto premises are located in the building that closes Rio terrà Lista di Spagna, named after the Catalan family that commissioned it in the 17th-18th century. The legend may or may not be true that the family was so rich it threw crockery away af-

(3)

ter each celebration, but it was certainly rich enough to entrust Giambattista Tiepolo with decoration of the salon; here the artist worked in 1746-47, enclosing in faux perspectives and architectures the frescoes depicting *Cleopatra's embarkation, the Banquet of Cleopatra and Anthony* **(3)**, *Allegories, Venus and Cupids, Winged Pegasus.*

14. San Giobbe

10-12 and 16-18

The Lombardo family played a prominent role in Venetian art and architecture between the 15th and 16th centuries; in particular, the city may thank two of its major figures, Pietro and Tullio Lombardo, for completion of the church located near the Tre Archi Bridge over Cannaregio canal. This place of worship was erected in the mid-15th century, ordered by Doge Cristoforo Moro, in a style that documents the evolution from Late Gothic to Renaissance. Both these styles cohabit in the façade and in the interior, which is outstanding for its sculptures and for masterpieces by Tuscan artists. First, however, you should visit the sacristy (with its wonderful triptych by Antonio Vivarini and Giovanni d'Alemagna, dated 1440-50) and observe the presbytery structure, already in full Renaissance flow. Then, along the left wall of the nave, you will find the Madonna or Martini chapel, opened by Antonio Rossellino: a splendid essay of Della Robbia art is the glazed multicoloured terracotta that holds medallions (both unique in this city).

15. The Ghetto

From 1516 to 1797 Venice's rich Jewish community was forced to reside in the Ghetto **(4)**, an expression whose exact origins are still uncertain (some sustaining that it

(4)

(1)

comes from the word *"getto"*, the molten metal produced in the foundries that were located here at one time; others say *"gettus"*, a term that indicated mooring points) but certainly coined on the Lagoon shores. The chosen area, of limited dimensions (located between Cannaregio canal and Rio della Misericordia, and between the Chioverette lanes and Rio Terrà San

(2)

Leonardo and Rio Farsetti), was "packed" to bursting point with 5,000 residents, explaining the unusually high buildings; the first to be established was Ghetto Nuovo (1516), extended in later times with Ghetto

Vecchio (1541 and 1589), and with Ghetto Nuovissimo (1633). Strolling along Fondamenta di Cannaregio, which cuts north-west on the Cannaregio canal, you will be quite near to the portico that served as access to the Ghetto and whose jambs still bear marks from the hinges for the doors that were once used to close off the area at night. Continuing you will enter **Ghetto Vecchio**, where Campiello delle Scuole is the site of two of the many Jewish schools dedicated to each national community forced to reside here: the Spanish and the Levantine **(1)**. Another public space is the Campiello del **Ghetto Nuovo**, with the **Jewish Museum**, or **Museo Ebraico (2)** *(Sun.-Fri. 10-19, Winter 10-16.30; multiple ticket to enter schools too)*, which illustrates

Jewish art during the period of confinement. This is also the location of Scuola Grande Tedesca, Scuola Grande del Canton and Scuola Grande Italiana.

16. Sant'Alvise
Mon.-Sat. 10-17

The bridge that crosses Rio della Misericordia is the exit from the Ghetto and leads to Fondamenta degli Ormesini, initially Calle della Malvasia, a straight stretch leading to a secluded church, virtually unknown to tourists. It is said to have been built by a Venetian noble woman, who became a nun after St Louis (Alvise is actually the Venetian "distortion" of the saint's name) appeared to her in a dream. Nowadays the church has a simple exterior and the interior was remodelled in the 17th century; there are some unexpected tempera panels dated 15th century and, surprisingly, some canvases by Giambattista Tiepolo on the right-hand wall and in the presbytery (splendid *Ascent to Calvary*).

17. Madonna dell'Orto
Mon.-Sat. 10-17

If the Tintoretto canvases in the Scuola Grande di San Rocco and neighbouring church whet your appetite, it is well worth visiting the church on the islet next door to Sant'Alvise. Or if you are looking for a crowd-free nook of Venice, do not miss a place of worship founded in the 1300s and

ebuilt the century after. This means that the façade **(3)** merges harmoniously with the Romanesque, Gothic and Renaissance elements that so eloquently document the portal. Inside the basilica, a theory of works by Tintoretto begins on the right wall, beyond the panel by Cima da Conegliano (1493c.). In point of fact, he painted the *Presentation of Mary in the Temple* (1552; San Mauro chapel), the *Last Judgement* and the *Adoration of the Golden Calf* (presbytery), as well as *t Agnes resuscitates icinius* (Contarini hapel).

18. Strada Nuova

f Piazza San Marco is he only public space in a Serenissima called a piazza", the only street alled such in Venice, is trada Nuova, laid in the mid-19th century to improve the section connecting the railway station to Rialto (which explains not so much its width as its unusual, traight track). You will realise you are in the treet because it is packed with tourists carrying suitcases.

19. Ca' d'Oro

Mon. 8.15-14;
Tue.-Sun. 8.15-19.15

Although little remains of the gilding, the façade of the Galleria Giorgio Franchetti building rightly appears as one of the most characteristic examples of Venetian Gothic (15th century). Arriving from Strada Nuova, you will first see the side of the Palazzo set on the canal, practically a minor prospect with crenellations on the wall, a handsome portal and windows. The main façade is actually near the water-bus jetty, split into a right-hand wall, with full masonry with single lights and windows, and to the left enhanced lower down by a portico and above by two loggias; the two sections are united by multicoloured marble decoration and, above, white stone crenellations.
A visit to the Galleria Giorgio Franchetti, a collection left by the Torinese musician, begins in the inner courtyard, closed on two sides by an arcade, decorated in the centre by a lovely well-curb, and is the starting point for a covered staircase supported by ogive arches. Although the museum is not enormous, it has some works that are mentioned by Italian art history manuals: a tempera on canvas *St Sebastian* that Mantegna painted in about 1506; a *double portrait* by Tullio Lombardo; a *Crucifixion* by Giovanni Boccati; two *Views* by Francesco Guardi **(4)**.

20. San Crisostomo

8.30-12.15 and 15.30-19
Sun. 10.15-12.15 e 15-19

Mauro Codussi's greatest creation is the church you will meet on the left after crossing Rio dei SS Apostoli, going towards Rialto. The architect worked on it from 1497-1504, creating a Renaissance style on a Greek cross plan. In harmony are the *Saints* by Giovanni Bellini (first altar to the right) and Sebastiano del Piombo's altarpiece (1509c.) in the presbytery.

(4)

Shopping

Were you to judge by the string of souvenirs and tacky goods that greet the tourist outside Santa Lucia railway station or near the Piazzale Roma and Tronchetto Island parking lots, you would think that buying anything authentically Venetian on the shores of the Lagoon is impossible. An impression confirmed by the proliferation of Italian and international top fashion designer boutiques along the streets that lead to the historic heart of the city: Le Mercerie, more than any other, underwent extreme changes in the range of business activities, with the historic shops elbowed out by glittering display windows showing goods no different to what could be found on sale in New York, Tokyo or Rome.

Fortunately not everything is lost, even what is described above is inevitably the price La

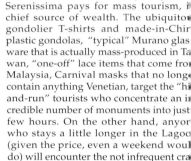

Serenissima pays for mass tourism, its chief source of wealth. The ubiquitous gondolier T-shirts and made-in-China plastic gondolas, "typical" Murano glassware that is actually mass-produced in Taiwan, "one-off" lace items that come from Malaysia, Carnival masks that no longer contain anything Venetian, target the "hit-and-run" tourists who concentrate an incredible number of monuments into just a few hours. On the other hand, anyone who stays a little longer in the Lagoon (given the price, even a weekend would do) will encounter the not infrequent craft shops, unexpectedly numerous costume jewellers, scores of windows packed with objects and paper that are all handmade, dozens of bookshops, antiquarians. Even if you don't intend to buy, it's still worth venturing inside, especially as you'll encounter this kind of business in an area of the city enjoying a reprieve from tourism: you may be lucky enough to watch the creation of a vogue bijou or a mask, or "lose yourself" amidst ship furniture and Art Deco objets. Nor should you be scared off by the prices – true to Venice's reputation as a costly city – because it is still possible to "get a bargain": a swirl of Burano lace, some Murano glass (a bead or a "murrina" [Murano glass bijoux] have that extra something if bought directly in the island's glassworks), or a gilt frame restored by an expert antiquarian.

Finally, some advice for anyone who wants to feel truly Venetian: go shopping in any of the markets held throughout the city.

Shopping

Apparel

*N*o lack of stores selling world-famous fashion labels but they certainly cannot be thought to be typical Venetian shops. Simply because you can find the same garments, belts, shoes on sale in many other cities all over the planet. Not so for lace, hats and fabrics.

Balocoloc
Santa Croce 2134,
Tel. 0415240551

A hatter that offers endless variations: from straw to La Serenissima's typical tricorn hat.

Gianni Dittura
Calle dei Fuseri, S. Marco 819
Tel. 0415223502

The place to buy "furlane" or "papesse", the Venetian version of Spanish espadrilles, so cal-

ed as they were invented in Friuli; they were once worn by gondoliers and servants but over the years have acquired their own image as unassuming footwear.

Jesurum
Cannaregio 3219, Fondamenta della Sensa; tel. 041.5242540

Since 1870 produces extraordinary lace and passing time has certainly not tarnished the tradition nor the quality in any way (*Tues.-Sat. 10-17*).

La Bottega di Cenerentola
Calle dei Saoneri, S. Polo 2721
Tel. 0415232006

Every imaginable type of lace and for every application and occasion.

Groceries

*E*ven in this third millennium, Venice is

Watch out for the addresses

If Venetian place-names have virtually no comparable forms in the rest of Italy, its street numbering in the addresses of stores, public premises, restaurants and hotels in the old centre is in itself *unique* across the peninsula. In point of fact, it does not advance with the calle, campiello, fondamento or rio, but essentially progresses according to the waterway within each of the city's six historic districts. That explains why it is quite normal to find four-figure street numbers in the Lagoon and also why it may well occur that two businesses directly opposite one another have completely unrelated numbers.

still able to astonish in this particular commodity sector: daily markets (not only on Rialto), heedless of tourists, often occupy extremely attractive locations, and with pontoons mooring in the wider rios to sell residents with fruit and vegetables.

Centro Studi di Storia del Tessuto e del Costume

To see exactly how refined La Serenissima's textile production was, and perhaps seek some suggestions for an elegant purchase, you can go straight to 18th-century Palazzo Mocenigo, which belonged to the famous family that gave Venice seven doges. This is the location of the Centro Studi di Storia del Tessuto e del Costume (Fabric and costume research centre) (*Tues.-Sun. 10-16, Summer 10-17*). The building still has many of its original furnishings, which offer a cross-section of the rooms where noble people lived from the 12th to the 18th century. There are also exhibits of costumes, accessories, fabrics and fashion plates.

Burano: lace island

When you mention lace in Venice you mean Burano, where the craft was introduced by La Serenissima's noblewomen in the 16th century. Nonetheless, the history of this scrap of land in the north of the Lagoon goes much further back and speaks of a far more important settlement, founded by refugees from Roman *Altinum* in the 6th century, developing only from the 12th century because of the neighbouring settlements of Mazzorbo and Torcello. Even today, anyone who sets off for Burano on the water-bus from Venice's Fondamenta Nuove, does so because

they personally want to see where La Serenissima's filmy lace is made, using a bobbin and single needle, with only "punti in aria" (stitches with no linen foundation) and guipure stitches, ignorant of the fact that this tradition risked extinction in the late 18th century, and was recovered only in the mid-1800s by foundation of a

special school. The glory of a truly refined art is celebrated precisely on the island by the Museo del Merletto or **Lace Museum** *(summer Wed.-Mon. 10-17; winter Wed.-Mon. 10-16)*, set up in a Gothic building in Piazza Galuppi: the Museum is unique not only for the product, which is documented here by a series of truly incredible uses (lace is found on collars, bedspreads,

handkerchiefs, tablecloths, doilies made between the 19th and 20th century), but also by the fact that you can watch the expert lacemakers at work, as they conjure up splendid masterpieces using famous Venezia and Murano stitches. Burano, however, is not just this traditional item. There are interesting fishermen's cottages, often still structured over two storeys with brightly-painted façades.
It is also worth popping into the main church, the 16th-century **San Martino** *(9-12 and 15-18)*, with an 18th-century leaning belfry and a Tiepolo *Crucifixion*.

Drogheria Mascari
Ruga degli Spezieri,
San Polo 381, Tel. 0415229762

Dried fruit, tea, pastries, wine and grappa in the only store on theme that survives in ancient Serenissima's "spice road", in the heart of Rialto district.

Panificio G. Volpe
Calle del Ghetto Vecchio,
Cannaregio 1143
Tel. 041715178

All products baked here are authentic traditional Jewish recipes: from almond-based pastries to unleavened bread.

Household goods and furniture

*W*hy not enhance your home with something purchased during a weekend at the Lagoon? An antique frame, an item of ship's furniture or some pottery?

Shopping

Alessandro Merlin
Calle del Pestrin,
Castello 3876
Tel. 0415225895

All pottery here is mostly black and white, and always it is even hand-made.

historic frame-makers, who will restore an old item or sell you a new one.

Bevilacqua
Fondamenta Canonica,
S. Marco 337/b; tel. 0415227581

Typical Venetian furnishing fabrics.

Canestrelli
Campiello Barbaro, Dorsoduro
364/a; tel. 0415227072

One of Venice's most

Carli
Corte Rotta, Castello 4725
Tel. 0415224155

If you want to furnish a room in sea-faring style, why not transform a handmade gondola rowlock into a precious knick-knack?

Cicogna
Campo San Tomà,
San Polo 2867
Tel. 0415227678

This is the third genera-tion of a Venetian family of wood restorers and gilders.

Fusetti Diego
Ghetto Vecchio,
Cannaregio 1219
Tel. 041720092

Jewish crafts, but also silver filigree and Mura-no stem glasses.

Mondonovo Maschere
Ponte dei Pugni,
Dorsoduro 3063
Tel. 0415287344

Very popular with film buffs as this is where Stanley Kubrick ordered the masks he used for his last film Eyes wide shut, and offering any-thing you might require for hiding your own face behind a counte-nance of bygone times, as well as providing a host of Carnival struc-tures and machines.

Saverio Pastor
Fondamenta Soranzo
detta Fornace,
Dorsoduro 341
Tel. 0415225699
e-mail: savepastor@libero.it

A craftsman applies the ancient oar-maker's art to produce the oar-pegs that are called "forcole" in the Lagoon area. The oar-pegs are so lovely and unique that they have become conscious-ly minimal furnishing accessories.

Shopping

VENETIA STVDIVM

Venetia Studium
Calle de le Ostreghe
San Marco 2428
Tel. 0415229859
www.venetiastudium.com

Clothing, accessories and furnishing accessories for refined tastes, hand-printed fabrics and Fortuny shades. For connoisseurs only!

Jewellery

*T*he right addresses for avoiding buying Venetian pearls that actually come from the Far East and jewels that are only traditional in appearance; but also information on where you can make some unusual purchases.

Daniele e Stefano Attombri
Sottoportico degli Orafi,
Rialto 74; tel. 0415212524

Look out for this jeweller who of those working only with antique pearls turns out some lovely

compositions using silver, iron and copper.

Gualti
Rio Terà Canal 3111, Dorsoduro
Tel. 0415201731

Gualti is a young artist who creates magnificent jewel-sculptures. Necklaces, earrings, brooches and accessories that combine vivid colours with delicate grace.

Herriz
Calle larga XXII Marzo,
San Marco 2381
Tel. 0415204276

A range of jewellery products that boasts splendid examples from the 1920s and 1930s.

Il Coccio di Marina
Salizada dei Greci,
Castello 3446
Tel. 0415285884

Would you prefer a unique necklace of its genre, such as one produced using authentic period pearls? This is the right store.

Missiaglia
Piazza San Marco, San Marco
125, Tel. 0415224464

Over the last 160 years this workshop has been producing craft designs using gold and gems to historic designs.

Perle e Dintorni
Calle della Mandola,
San Marco 3740
Calle della Bissa,
San Marco 5468
S. Polo 2102/a;
tel. 0415205068

Beads, but also everything else you need to string necklaces.

Book stores and stationers

*T*he city that can boast illustrious sons such as Marco Polo and Carlo Goldoni, was also the location for some of Italy's earliest printers, so the art of printing and paper is quite at home here. Despite the tourists, you can still find lots of shops with rarities and curios, as well as bookbinders and workshops that make marble-paper and writing paper, as well as ex-libris stamps.

Shopping

Alberto Valese
Campo S. Stefano,
S. Marco 3471
Te. 0415238830
www.albertovalese-ebru.com

Graphomaniacs will find all they need to feed their passion here: customised writing paper – and gift wrap –, nibs in all shapes and hardness, inks of all types and colours, and even sealing wax.

Antica Legatoria Piazzesi
Campiello de la Feltrina,
San Marco 2511/c
Tel. 0415221202
www.legatoriapiazzesi.it

Marble-paper in note-books, address books but also single sheets in fantastic patterns and lots of designs; several products are made with 18th-century prints.

Fantoni
Salizada S. Luca,
S. Marco 4121
Tel. 0415220700

Extremely well-stocked, especially with art pub-lications.

Gianni Basso
Calle del Fumo,
Cannaregio 5306
Tel. 0415234681

This really is a workshop of times past, a stone's throw from Fondamenta Nuove, where you can order bookplates, visiting cards and writing paper, following the trend set by the illustrious clients (of-ten foreigners) who made the store famous.

Il Fontego
Campo San Bartolomeo,
San Marco 5361
Tel. 0415200470

Rare or even very old books, near Fondaco dei Tedeschi, opposite Rial-to Bridge.

Libreria Filippi
San Lio,
Castello 5763
Tel. 0415235635
Casselleria,
Castello 5284
Tel. 0415236916
e-mail: filippi@doge.it

A publisher-bookseller with one thing on his mind: the city's curiosi-ties and traditions, where you find out everything and more about place names, Car-nival and even about well-curbs in the little squares.

Mare di Carta
Fondamenta dei Bolentini,
Santa Croce 222
Tel. 041716304
www.maredicarta.it

All you need for famili-arising with the sea in an area where tourists rarely venture in Venice (the store is actually near the church of San Nicolò da Tolentino and the University); Italian, French and English books, magazines, calen-dars and heaps of nauti-cal maps.

Paolo Olbi
Cannaregio 5478/a;
Campo Santa Maria Nuo-va, Cannaregio 6061
Calle della Mandola,
San Marco 3653
Tel. 0415285025

Pride and joy of these three stores, linked to a busy bookbind-ery, is the special paper,

53

produced with the ancient vat method; lovely address books and diaries, which are also available with leather covers.

Glass

A *lthough you really should mistrust the string of objects stamped "original Murano" displayed on stalls and in shops, that doesn't mean you won't be able to make the right purchases in this sector. Even without going out to the island's glassworks.*

Archimede Seguso
Piazza San Marco 143
Tel. 0415289041

Famous worldwide for production of art that is outstanding for style and technique.

Pauly & C.
Palazzo Trevisan Cappello
Ponte dei Consorzi 4391/A
Tel. 0415209899

Ancient and prestigious glassworks established in 1866. There are authentic works of art to be admired in the smart store windows that look out onto Piazza San Marco and in the 16th-century rooms of Palazzo Trevisan Cappello, Venice's largest collection of Murano glass. Visits by appointment.

Vittorio Costantini
Calle del Fumo,
Cannaregio 5311
Tel. 0415222265

Inspired by Murano and Lagoon fauna and flora this master glassblower produces birds, insects, fish and flowers, and continues to work with the extremely refined and rare flame technique (the liquid material is poured into tubes of different diameters and colours, which are moulded by heating).

Sweets for each month

A "side effect" of the Crusades to the Holy Land was the arrival of sugar in Venice. This makes it easy to understand why the city abounds with so many typical pastries, often linked to religious and lay holidays. For instance, everyone knows *"baicoli"*, which look like ultra slim sweet flour hosts.

Then there are the less familiar *"zaleti"* made with maize flour and raisins, *"bussolai"* which are s-shaped or round, *"pane dei Dogi"* made with almonds and currants, *"moro"* filled with cocoa, almonds and candied peel, *"nosea"* made with hazelnuts chocolate, or sweet *"fugassa"*. At Carnival you will find not only *"fritole"* with pinenuts and raisins, but also *"galani"* and *"castagnole"*. Autumn specialities are *"mostaccioli di Sant'Erasmo"* made with must and gelatine, *"fave"* with sugar and pine-nuts, as well as the *"San Martino"*, made either with quince jam or from short pastry covered in chocolate.

Shopping

Markets and Fairs

Venice has a tradition lost in the mists of time: the markets that are held daily or weekly in various points throughout the city. They still offer a typically Venetian atmosphere, with the vendors hawking their goods loudly in the dialect of Carlo Goldoni. Then there are the fairs, in part rooted in religious festivities, whereas the antiques markets tend to be more for tourists.

Rialto Market
Rialto, S. Polo (Mon.-Sat.)
Venetians and tourists mingle between Le Pescherie and Rialto Bridge, in their quest for fruit and vegetables at accessible prices, or the freshest fish. There are lots of stalls selling these three types of goods, whilst the grocers behind them sell a range of typical local items.

Santa Margherita Market
Campo S. Margherita, Dorsoduro (Mon.-Sat)
Fruit, vegetables, fish, every day in a Dorsoduro square near the Carmini and Ca' Foscari University.

Rio Terrà Market
Campo S. Leonardo, Cannaregio (Mon.-Sat.)
Fruit and vegetables only, but really fresh, in the Cannaregio *sestiere*, along the route that connects the railway station to the Rialto area, a stone's throw from the glittering air of Palazzo Vendramin-Calergi and its casino.

Madonna della Salute Fair
Campo Santa Maria della Salute
On 20 and 21 November, the parvis of the basilica designed by Baldassarre Longhena becomes a massive open-air market, another commemoration of the end of the late 16th-century plague.

Santa Lucia Fair
Campo San Geremia
It is traditional in the Veneto region to celebrate Saint Lucy and the "shortest day there is" (12 and 13 Dec.). This all happens on the Cannaregio shore of the Lagoon, opposite Palazzo Labia and its Tiepolo masterpieces.

Miracoli Market
Campo Santa Maria Nova
Six times a year a bric-a-brac market is set up near the Santa Maria dei Miracoli church in the Castello district.

Antiques Market
Campo San Maurizio
In the week before Easter and for the feasts of the Ascension and St Maurice, as well as for Christmas, this San Marco district square changes appearance turning from a thoroughfare to a huge display case.

Santo Stefano Market
Campo Santo Stefano
Venetian craft products on sale in this San Marco district square from 1-24 December every year.

Masks and mask-makers Market
Campo Santo Stefano
Everything you want and need for Carnival "under false pretences".

Shopping

Murano: glass island

Today's 70 glassworks "say it all" about the close links between Murano and the production of glass since the art of blowing incandescent raw material was established here in 1291. It was actually a doge's decree that year that ordered transfer of the glassworks that until then had been in Venice, to Murano: a decision made necessary by the fire risks created in what was virtually a wooden city at that time; the decision was accompanied by privileges that intended to "compensate" the artisans who moved, ensuring that their production never suffered a crisis. Again, in the case of Murano, its history goes back further than 1291 and

presents analogies with that of Burano (refugees from Roman *Altinum* in the 6th century actually moved to San Donato island, one of the five now occupied by Murano, although the area is famed as a sort of "Little Venice": it has its own Grand Canal and a dense network of alleys. No tourist wants to miss the glassworks – where you can see the glass being blown and the most prestigious items in annexed museums (remember the excellent names in local production, like Barovier and

Toso, Nason Moretti, Seguso, Salviati) and make purchases – however the **Glass Museum (Museo del Vetro)** is also packed *(Apr.-Oct., Thu.-Tues. 10-17; Nov.-Mar., Thu.-Tues. 10-16)*, where the history of glass is narrated in various key themes: splendid historic examples (impossible not to mention the 15th-century Barovier cup), the different production techniques, the evolution of styles. The marvellous transparencies of the glassware

sings "counterpoint" to the silhouette of the nearby **basilica of SS. Maria e Donato** *(Mon.-Sat. 9-12 and 15.30-19, Sun. 15.30-19)*, founded in the 7th century; the apse is the most interesting part of the exterior, both for the refined combined presence of Ravenna, Romanesque and oriental elements, and for the elegant play of solids and hollows; the nave and two-aisle interior, with its 1140 mosaic floor, is followed by the apse bowl with a 13th-century floor and an altarpiece (St Donatus, 1310) by Paolo Veneziano. Very significant is also the nearby **church of San Pietro Martire** *(8.30-12 and 15.30-19)*, built in the 14th century, but remodelled in the two following centuries: the Gothic interior, with a nave and two aisles and three apses, is furnished chiefly with works brought from suppressed religious complexes, including two important canvases (1510-13 and 1488) by Giovanni Bellini.

Restaurants

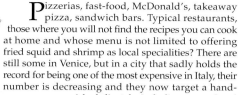

Pizzerias, fast-food, McDonald's, takeaway pizza, sandwich bars. Typical restaurants, those where you will not find the recipes you can cook at home and whose menu is not limited to offering fried squid and shrimp as local specialities? There are still some in Venice, but in a city that sadly holds the record for being one of the most expensive in Italy, their number is decreasing and they now target a hand-picked clientele, including on one hand incurable gourmets and on the other foreigners with limit-free credit cards. To be honest, it isn't necessary to spend a fortune for a meal: the bill will certainly be big if you choose a famous restaurant, because you do pay for the location and service; but if you "make do" with trattorias and choose carefully (typical eateries have a limited range, local recipes and make few concessions to tourism), the quality/price ratio probably won't be all in favour of the customer, but you should come away satisfied. You will also discover that even if Venetian cuisine is prevalently fish-based, there is also a strong use of vegetables and rustic ingredients like rice and polenta.

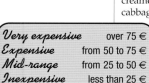

Those of you who think that "cicheti" can only be sampled with a "spritz" or an "ombra" will be surprised. A typical Venetian meal begins with hors d'oeuvres: endless samples of scallops, "canoce lesse" (boiled mantis crab), "schie" (Lagoon shrimp), spider-crab, fried "moleche" (crabs), "sarde in saor" (marinate pilchards dressed with onion, raisins and pine nuts) and "bovoleti" (snails in garlic). If you enjoy first courses, perhaps you should skip the starters and try: "risi e bisi" (rice and peas), at one time the main course offered by the Doges at their banquets and whose recipe was linked to the feast day of St Mark; "bigoli", flour and semolina spaghetti in sauce or with duck ragout; meat-based broths (tripe is the main ingredient) or fish-based soups (razor clams are the main ingredient). Maize polenta is served both with fish (from stuffed squid to cuttlefish in ink, from pilchards to creamed salt cod) and with meat (pork ribs with Savoy cabbage, Venetian-style liver, stuffed duck). Of the vegetables, don't miss "castraure" artichokes from Sant'Erasmo island, and of the desserts the tiramisù, however much it is now seen as a national dish. And to help you digest it all, what better than a "gropin", a lemon sorbet with a touch of vodka or, better still, prosecco.

Very expensive	over 75 €
Expensive	from 50 to 75 €
Mid-range	from 25 to 50 €
Inexpensive	less than 25 €

Restaurants

A compass for Venetian recipes

A mini glossary of Venetian specialities that will help you choose, especially useful when you are eating in trattorias with menus only in dialect, or chalked up on a blackboard.

Bacalà mantecà	Creamed salt cod
Baicoli	Biscuit slivers
Bisi	Peas
Bussolai buranei	Egg biscuits – either round or S-shaped
Castradina	Mutton with Savoy cabbage
Crostoi	Chiacchiere biscuits
Figà a la venexiana	Venetian-style liver
Fritole	Fritters
Luganega	Long, thin sausage
Panada	Soup with bread, garlic, oil, laurel and Parmesan
Pastissada	Mixture of vegetable, cheese, cured meats and pasta bound with polenta
Peoci	Mussels
Pinsa	A pastry made with flour, aniseed, raisins, dried figs and candied fruit
Stracaganase	Dried chestnuts
Soppressa	Fresh salami
Veneziana	Brioche pastry covered with chopped almonds and granulated sugar

Very expensive

Ai Gondolieri
San Vio, Dorsoduro 366
Tel. 0415286396
www.aigondolieri.com

Opposite the Peggy Guggenheim Collection; specialities include Veneto meat and desserts; all served in an elegant yet informal atmosphere.

Ai Mercanti
Calle dei Fuseri,
San Marco 4346/a
Tel. 0415238369

A small court in a secluded area of the *sestiere* acts as the entrance to an elegant restaurant offering some of Venice's most typical dishes.

Antico Martini
Campo San Fantin,
San Marco 1983
Tel. 0415224121
www.anticomartini.com

A place to meet before or after a performance at nearby La Fenice, offering classic meat and fish-based recipes in an elegant ambience full of history.

Antico Pignolo
Calle degli Specchieri,
San Marco 451
Tel. 0415228321
e-mail: anticopignolo@libero.it

With its elegant and sophistication, this restaurant is definitely a high-class choice – both for the menu (fish specialities from both traditional and innovative recipes) and for the wine-cellar, which includes superlative labels and vintages.

Cipriani
Fondamenta San Giovanni,
Giudecca 10
Tel. 0415207744
www.hotelcipriani.it

Dinner on the restaurant's panoramic terrace, annexed to the Cipriani Hotel, is strongly recommended for all romantics; traditional Venetian cooking with fish and first courses as a speciality.

Club del Doge
Campo San Maria del Giglio,
San Marco 2467
Tel. 041794611
www.luxurycollection.com/
grittipalace

At the Hotel Gritti Palace you can lunch or dine – and even enjoy its panoramic terrace – on classic dishes and also on traditional Venetian recipes.

Al Covo

Campiello della Pescheria,
Castello 3968
Tel. 0415223812

There is a prevalence of fish in this restaurant, offering recherché Veneto cuisine in a rustic atmosphere.

Da Arturo

Calle degli Assassini,
San Marco 3656
Tel. 0415286974

A charming trattoria where you can try meat and vegetable dishes.

Da Fiore

Calle del Scaletèr,
San Polo 2202
Tel. 041721308
www.dafiore.com

First course and fish as per local tradition, in an elegant and charming ambience; the wine list offers the best companions for the menu.

Da Ivo

Calle dei Fuseri,
San Marco 1809
Tel. 0415285004

In this restaurant serving Venetian specialities alongside Tuscan recipes using mushrooms and truffles, you may well be the only non-Venetian being served.

alla Zanze

Santa Croce 213,
Tel. 0415223555

Venetian-style fish excellent spaghetti with Venus

clams - caparosoli) in a historic palazzo, where you can watch the chefs at work; only Veneto and Friuli wines.

Do Forni

Calle degli Specchieri,
San Marco 468
Tel. 0415232148
www.doforni.it

Sample specialities of typical Venetian cuisine as if you were in a restaurant car (the dining room is actually fitted out like the famous Orient Express).

Gran Caffè Quadri

Piazza San Marco 120
Tel. 0415222105
www.quadrivenice.com

Lunch and supper with a fish menu in the famous shore restaurant opposite Caffè Florian, and enhanced by ceramics, silver and Murano glass.

Harry's Bar

Calle Vallaresso,
San Marco 1323
Tel. 0415285777

Given the bar's fame, linked quite some time ago to the famous Bellini, lunches and dinners are now served, with classic dishes of Veneto cuisine that offer mainly fish and first courses.

La Caravella

Calle larga XXII Marzo,
San Marco 2397
Tel. 0415208901
www.hotelsaturnia.it

Specialities of Veneto cuisine offered in unusual ambience: in winter a dining room resembling a caravel bridge; in summer, the 14th-century courtyard.

La Colomba

Piscina di Frezzeria,
San Marco 1665
Tel. 0415221175

One of Venice's historic restaurants where you can enjoy traditional regional cuisine in a dining room

Restaurants

Torcello: where Venice was "born"

Not even Ernest Hemingway was immune to the charm of Torcello, the island that had been settled by refugees from Roman Altino fleeing from the fury of the barbarian invasions, bringing with them the bishop of their town, which later moved to the island of San Pietro and was destined to become the bishopric of Venice-to-be. A visit to Torcello is suggested – like a virtual reality game – as a sort of journey back in time to the earliest history of La Serenissima. The island seems to have stood still in time, rooted in the "glorious era" of the Dark Ages, when it boasted over 20,000 inhabitants; nevertheless, its importance ran a short course and after its foundation in the 5th century, developing existing settlements, in the 8th-9th century it began to decline, turning into a gigantic quarry for the construction of Venice. The builders furiously "recycled" so much that only two places of worship have survived of the ancient settlement. Not a great deal, really, but extraordinarily important. When you arrive with the water-bus, coasting the right of Canale dei Borgognoni, which ends at Piazza Santa Fosca, you are in the location of the island's surviving monuments. The **Cathedral** *(10-17; Summer 10.30-18)* belfry is visible even at a distance, with its hollow square bell chamber. The place of worship was founded in 639 by Esarcio, Exarch of Ravenna (documented by an inscription to the left of the high altar), making it the oldest church in the Lagoon. It was extended in 824 and partially rebuilt in 1008: the façade is extremely simple and is connected to the neighbouring church of Santa Fosca by a narthex; the plain interior – a nave and two aisles with three apses – is a backdrop to sequences of Venetian-Byzantine mosaics (12th-13th century): the most important is the *Universal Judgement* covering the counter-façade, but there is also a splendid *Madonna and Child* on gold background in the apse bowl, not to mention the compositions in the chapel to the right of the main church. The neighbouring **church of Santa Fosca** *(10-12.30 and 14-18.30)* also proves the extremely close links between Torcello and Ravenna. It seems that the church's floor plan originally resembled the San Vitale complex when it was built in the 11th-12th centuries (intended to house the remains of the local saint) with a Greek cross layout, pentagonal presbytery and cross vault under a dome roof. Relics brought to light on the island are in **Torcello's museum** *(March-Oct., Tues.-Sun. 10.30-17; Nov.-Feb., Tues.-Sun. 10-16.30)*, which narrates the history of the settlement through remains dating from the Etruscan era to the 16th century.

---

decked with modern paintings.

La Corte Sconta
Calle del Pestrin,
Castello 3886
Tel. 0415227024

Surf only (fish but shellfish and seafood too) in a cheerful atmosphere.

Taverna la Fenice
Campiello della Fenice,
San Marco 1939
Tel. 0415223856
www.tavernalafenice.com

Right next door to the famous La Fenice opera house and a favourite with actors and theatre-goers who want to sample Veneto cooking.

Expensive

Agli Alboretti
Rio Terrà Foscarini,
Accademia 884
Tel. 0415230058

Italian fish-based cuisine and first course offered in an ambience that is at its best in summer, when the chef's specials are served under a pergola that valorises the atmosphere of the restaurant.

Restaurants

Ai Frati
Fondamenta Venier 4,
Murano
Tel. 041736694

An old convent, in the centre of the island, for sampling typical Venetian lagoon, fish-based cuisine.

Ai Quattro Feri
Calle lunga San Barnaba,
Dorsoduro 2754/a
Tel. 0415206978

Veneto cuisine offering both meat and fish dishes, served in a simple scenario.

Al Bacareto
San Samuele,
San Marco 3447
Tel. 0415289336

Popular above all with visitors to nearby Palazzo Grassi, offering typical Venetian and Veneto dishes.

Al Gatto Nero
Fondamenta della Giudecca
88, Burano,
Tel. 041730120
www.gattonero.com

This trattoria is set on the canal front and serves simple, prevalently fish-based cuisine.

Al Graspo de Ua
Calle dei Bombaseri,
San Marco 5094
Tel. 0415200150

One of Venice's historic eating places, with elegant, intimate ambience and serving a combination of local dishes, Italian and international recipes.

Al Ponte del Diavolo
Via Borgognoni 10/11,
Torcello, Tel. 041730401

A rustic restaurant along the street that links the water-bus stop to the Santa Fosca district, serving Veneto cuisine and with open-air seating.

Altanella
Calle delle Erbe, Giudecca 268,
Tel. 0415227780

The same family has run this restaurant for generations, ensuring that the menu loses none of is traditional flavour.

Antica Besseta
Salizada de Ca' Zusto,
Santa Croce 1395,
Tel. 041721687
www.yeaah.com/
anticabesseta

In a historic building near the railway station, Venetian and Veneto fish-based specialities.

Antica Carbonera
Calle Bembo,
San Marco 4648
Tel. 0415225479

For those who prefer to sample traditional Venetian dishes in an ambience hallmarked by the passion of the artists working around the Lagoon.

Bentigodi
Cannaregio 1423
Tel. 041716269

Traditional Venetian menu and wines, with a counter offering an endless selection of "cicheti" appetisers.

Restaurants

Fiaschetteria Toscana
Salizada San Giovanni Crisostomo, Cannaregio 5719 Tel. 0415285281

Despite the Tuscan name, it actually serves excellent Venetian fish-based dishes and has a vast range of wines.

La Favorita
Via Duodo 33, Lido Tel. 0415261626

Lagoon specialities that can be enjoyed under a pergola during the summer season.

Le Bistrot de Venise
Calle dei Fabbri, San Marco 4685 Tel. 0415236651 www.bistrotdevenise.com

This eatery offers traditional Venetian dishes in a historic building, decorated like a Parisian bistrot; extensive wine list.

Locanda Cipriani
Piazza Santa Fosca 29, Torcello. Tel. 041730150

Refined cuisine in a restaurant whose customers included Ernest Hemingway.

Il Sole sulla Vecia Cavana
Rio Terrà SS. Apostoli, Cannaregio 4642, Tel. 0415287106

Specialities of Venice and creative dishes prepared with almost obsessive attention to ingredients; excellent wine list.

Romano
Piazza Galuppi 221, Burano Tel. 041730030

Strictly traditional and only fish-based menu, served in rooms decorated with paintings by 20th-century artists.

San Tomà
Campo San Tomà, San Polo 2864; tel. 0415238819

For those who are looking for charm, check the classic cuisine served in a smart ambience tucked away far from the maddening crowds of Venice.

Mid-range

Al Leon d'Oro
Rio Terà della Maddalena Cannaregio 2345; tel. 041720693

A welcoming little restaurant where you can sample typical Venetian cuisine with the accent on seafood, from gnocchi with crabmeat to stuffed squid nesting in polenta and a tris of stockfish, to conclude with delicious home-made desserts.

Bancogiro
Campo San Giacometto, San Polo 122; tel. 0415232061

Only fish in this eatery in the heart of Rialto, near the Banco Giro portico (from which it takes its name).

Ca' d'Oro
Ramo Ca' d'Oro, Cannaregio 3912; tel. 0415285324

Open in the evenings, this tavern, also known as Alla Vedova, offers food and delicacies. You will have to book in advance.

Da Ignazio
Calle Saoneri, San Polo 2749, Tel. 0415234852

Anyone seeking Venet-

Wines

Not everyone knows that Venice is a wine city. Thanks to the island of Sant'Erasmo, where a small number of vines produce a quite difficult to find wine. So, traditional dishes must be accompanied by Veneto wines: Verona, Vicenza and Treviso reds and whites, which include Valpolicella and Merlot, Soave and Tocai. The spumante sector is located between Valdobbiadene and Conegliano, ideal aperitifs but also suitable with some dishes; pastries are enhanced with a sip of "vin santo".

ian look and feel in a restaurant should try this one, where the cuisine – the chef only prepares lagoon traditional recipes – is still that of the old trattorias, served in a courtyard garden.

Rioba
Fondamenta della Misericordia, Cannaregio 2553
Tel. 0415244379

Rioba is the name of one of the four Moors immortalised in the statues along the fondamenta of the same name. The restaurant is named after the Moor and has a typical Venetian menu, confirmed by the presence of many fish dishes, not a great deal of meat, and served outdoors in summer.

Vecio Fritolin
Calle della Regina, S. Croce 2262
Tel. 0415222881

Traditional fish menu near Ca' Corner della Regina. Don't miss the takeaway "scartosso de pesse".

Economical

Al Ponte La patatina
Calle Saoneri, S. Polo 2741/a,
Tel. 0415237238

This is a simple trattoria where you are sure to enjoy great fish-based dishes.

Alla Rivetta
Ponte S. Provolo, Castello 4625
Tel. 0415287302

If you don't have time to wait for a table, just

"quench" your appetite with lots of "cicheti", served at the counter with wine or "ombre".

Da Pampo
Calle Chinotto, Castello 24
Tel. 0415208419

Trattoria on Sant'Elena island, great for a pause if the stroll along the banks overlooking the San Marco canal continues past the Biennale, in an area that is simple but extremely charming; the speciality is a fish pie.

Gam-Gam
Calle del Ghetto Vecchio 1123
Tel. 041715284

Near the Ghetto Vecchio portico, which is one of the gateways to the area where Venetian Jews were forced to live for centuries, you

will find a place with a charming atmosphere serving great kosher food.

Osteria La Zucca
Campo del Megio, Santa Croce 1762
Tel. 0415241570

In a zone off the beaten tourist track (near the church of San Giacomo dell'Orio), a trattoria offering traditional dishes, ethnic cooking and lots of seasonal vegetable dishes; good selection of wines, with focus on Friuli labels.

Taverna San Trovaso
Dorsoduro 1016
Tel. 0415203703

A tasty fish dish or a good pizza near the Gallerie dell'Accademia.

Dai Tosi
Secco Marina, Castello 738
Tel. 0415237016

Trattoria-pizzeria in the Castello district, still popular for appearance and atmosphere.

Coffee and more

Coffee, music and performing arts

Beer cellars, pubs, snack bars have sprouted like mushrooms in recent years. Observing them you might be tempted to think that La Serenissima has sold her soul for her chief source of wealth: tourism. "typical" places where thousands of foreigners and Italians find music, colours and local products, have spread like wildfire, especially in the key areas for the classic tour of the Lagoon city, to the detriment of the small – let's say often tiny – businesses

where you could once find yourself plunged into a conversation in strong dialect of which you understood not a word. Objectively, it is quite difficult to experience this alienation nowadays, unless you are lucky enough to meet someone who still lives in Venice and will take you by the hand to unearth establishments in the old style. Yes, there are still some around, and if you have the good fortune to bump into one, the first thing you feel is marvel, followed immediately by the thought that you should keep it to yourself, to avoid "modernity" wiping it out.

Ironically, due to the very nature of the citizens who love to chat and the customs discovered by Venice's many merchants during their travels and trading, the city of the Doges was one of the first in Italy to install so-called coffee shops, which appeared after the arrival of Turkish coffee from much-hated Istanbul (it is said that the *Gran Caffè Quadri* was the first to serve it): the first was opened in 1683 and was such a success that

in less than a century another 200 followed suit. Luckily this tradition has not been lost and the proof is the presence of historic spots like *Florian, Quadri* and *Lavina*, not to mention their excellent imitators like Arrigo Cipriani's Harry's Bar (and its legendary Bellini cocktail).

Nonetheless, what really makes Venice unique is the *bacaro*: a tavern where you can have a glass of wine (which the Venetians call an "ombra") with an appetizer (or "cicheto" in dialect). This particular type of establishment is really only a couple of hundred years old, as it was invented hot on the heels of the city's annexation to the Kingdom of Italy: legend has it that a merchant from Trani decided to send wine from Puglia to the Lagoon area and the wine was so strong that the locals immediately christened it "vino da bacaro" (wine for whooping it up).

Coffee and more

What to eat and drink in a "bacaro"

The "spritz" is the undisputed queen of Venetian aperitifs, becoming famous after the Austrian acquisition of the former Serenissima after the Congress of Vienna in 1815; it was probably invented in Vienna and came to the Lagoon as a mix of white wine and soda water, later modified to offer two versions: the bitter option with Bitter Campari, the sweet option using Aperol. Peach pulp and DOC Prosecco are the ingredients for a Bellini: simple ingredients but only a few bars –

apart from the well-known *Harry's Bar*, of course – offer a good version. In Venice these drinks – or even a simple, more austere "ombra", in other words a glass of white, even sparkling wine – are served with equally famous "cicheti", appetisers that bear no resemblance to crisps and peanuts, but are deeply rooted in ancient culinary tradition. We can't list them all but they range from fried whitebait to cheese morsels, triangles of polenta and braised baby squid, slices of salami and grilled ink-fish; not to mention the vegetables (the artichokes grown on the island of Sant'Erasmo are famous even though they are quite rare) served pickled, stewed, fresh and grilled. That's why, in Venice, an aperitif can turn into a full meal!

Bacari

A la Campana
Calle dei Fabbri, S. Marco 4720
Tel. 0415285170

A nook of old Venice, a pleasant atmosphere, at the back of Rialto.

Ai Do Ladroni
Campo San Bartolomeo,
San Marco 5362

Sandwiches and typical dishes at the top of the street connecting Rialto with the railway station.

Ai Nomboli
Calle Goldoni,
San Polo 2717
Tel. 0415230955

Near Goldoni's house and the museum, a selection of the sandwiches with the filling Venice is famous for, even beyond the city limits.

Ai Postali
Fondamenta Rio Marin,
S. Polo 821; tel. 041715156

Exquisite bruschetta and crêpes near to the church of San Simeon Grande.

Ai Rusteghi
Campo San Bartolomeo,
San Marco 5529

Excellent wine to wash down the great sandwiches, in a tavern near Rialto.

Al Bacco
Fondamenta delle Capucine
Cannaregio 3054
Tel. 041721415

A typical Venetian tavern serving traditional dishes accompanied by Veneto wines.

Al Mascaron
Calle lunga S. Maria Formosa,,
Castello 5525 Tel. 0415225995

A tavern but with cooked meals too, for a typical dish to enjoy before or after visiting the church of San Zaccaria in Castello.

MASCARON
O S T E R I A

Coffee and more

All'Arco
Calle dell'arco, San Polo 436
Tel. 0415205666

Great "cicheti" and "ombre" in this spot near Rialto.

Alla Fontana
Fondamenta Cannaregio 1102

Taste some of the best "cicheti" in Cannaregio.

Al Ponte La patatina
Calle Saoneri, S. Polo 2741/a,
Tel. 0415237238

All kinds of vegetables, cooked in lots of ways at the counter of this eatery near the Scuola Grande di San Rocco.

Alle Testiere
Calle del Mondo Novo,
Castello 5801
Tel. 0415227220

Finger food and tasty dishes in a tavern located in a *sestiere* that still has some mysterious corners; the cooking is a sort of re-reading of Venetian culinary tradition, with some specialities in the main courses.

Antiche Cantine Arenghi
Calle della Testa,
Cannaregio 6369
Tel. 0415237691

Try a tasty Venetian dish here, near the SS. Giovanni e Paolo basilica.

Antico Dolo
Ruga Rialto, San Polo 778
Tel. 0415226546

Tripe, "rissa", "crostini", polenta and salt cod in the Rialto area.

Bomba
Calle dell'Oca,
Cannaregio 4297
Tel. 0415237452

An "ombra" and a "cicheto" near Campo SS. Apostoli and Strada Nuova.

Ca' d'Oro
Ramo Ca' d'Oro,
Cannaregio 3912-3952
Tel. 0415285324

Also known as Alla Vedova, ideal for aperitifs, which can turn into a real appe-tite-quenching snack given the quantity of "cicheti" offered on the counter.

Cantina Vecia Carbonera
Rio Terà Maddalena,
Cannaregio 2329
Tel. 041710376

A "Grand Tour" of Venice's "bacari" must include a stop here.

Cantinone già Schiavi
Fondamenta Nani,
Dorsoduro 992, Tel.
0415230034

After the marvels of the Gallerie dell'Accademia,

get your strength up with a snack and an "ombra" here.

Da Dante
Corte Nova,
Castello 2877
Tel. 0415286163

The very Venetian tavern near the Arsenale.

Da Gigio
Fondamenta San Felice,
Cannaregio 3628/a
Tel. 0415285140

Wine by the glass even at the table, perhaps to wash down some typical traditional dishes.

Da Pinto
Campo Beccarie,
S. Polo 367
Tel. 0415224599

Where real Venetians hang out, after shopping at Rialto market, with a glass of prosecco and the "crostini" famous all over the city.

Do Mori
Calle dei Do Mori,
S.Polo 429
Tel. 0415225401

One of the oldest and most famous in Venice for the wine and "cicheti" on offer.

Do Spade
Calle Do Spade, S. Polo 860
Tel. 0415210574

Even Casanova was attracted to this "bacaro", seduced by the "ombre" and "cicheti" that also include game appetisers.

Leon Bianco
Salizada San Luca,
San Marco 4153

For a quick snack but also for a typical dish to sit down and enjoy at leisure.

Paradiso Perduto
Fondamenta
della Misericordia 2540
Tel. 041720581

In a charming corner of the Cannaregio area, you can enjoy food and jazz.

Promessi Sposi
Calle dell'Oca,
Cannaregio 4367
Tel. 0415228609

Very popular, just a stroll from Campo SS. Apostoli.

Bars and coffee shops

Algiubagiò
Fondamenta Nuove,
Cannaregio 5039

A moment to relax, sit at table in the open and enjoy the view of San Michele and Murano islands.

CAFFÉ FLORIAN

All'Angolo
Campo Santo Stefano,
San Marco 3464

Offers a vast choice of sandwiches, famous for great and abundant fillings.

Caffè Florian
Piazza San Marco 56
Tel. 0415285388

This really needs no introduction, one of the historic bars of Venice, opened in the Procuratie Nuove arcades in distant 1720; once the editorial office of the "Gazzetta veneta", this is where the 1848 uprisings began, where Venetian and foreign literati and intellectuals met. It is extremely expensive but it is worth visiting; if money is not short, sit and listen to the orchestra playing classic music – it's a must.

Coffee and more

Causin
Campo Santa Margherita, Dorsoduro 2996

Lovely ice creams, to linger over while you observe the rituals of the fruit and vegetable market opposite.

Da Nico
Dorsoduro 922
Tel. 0415225293

Famous mainly amongst Venetians for the so-called "gianduiotto da passeggio" and cream in ice, specialities to enjoy while looking out at Giudecca island, opposite.

Florian Artecaffè
Campiello Querini Stampalia, Castello 5252

An ideal place for a rest inside Palazzo Querini Stampalia, great after visiting the picture gallery, where the foundation often organises receptions for their cultural projects.

Gran Caffè Quadri
Piazza San Marco,
San Marco 120
Tel. 0415289299-5222105
www.quadrivenice.com

Opposite Caffè Florian (actually located in the Procuratie Vecchie arcades since the 19th century) and competing both for customers and for the honour of having been the first to bring Turkish coffee to the Lagoon. Like its competitor, it has an orchestra and very high prices.

Harry's Bar
Calle Vallaresso,
San Marco 1323
Tel. 0415285777

To sample the only real, original Bellini, this is where you have to go, because the aperitif was invented by the creative Arrigo Cipriani. Behind the Ala Napoleonica, it is simultaneously one of Venice's sacred locations frequented by political and show business figures, but it is also a bar for tasting great appetisers. As long as you aren't short of money.

Il Caffè
Campo Santa Margherita, Dorsoduro 2963

A historic address, to help you "recover" from the marvels of the Carmini complex, in a retro ambience created with marble and wall mirrors.

Margaret Duchamp
Campo Santa Margherita, Dorsoduro 3019

When it isn't packed with stallholders from the fruit and vegetable market opposite, it's packed with university students from Ca' Foscari.

Piero e Mauro
Calle dei Fabbri,
San Marco 881

A place just a short step from San Marco, furnished completely with ship's fixtures and offering famous Venetian sandwiches, washed down with an international assortment of beers.

Coffee and more

Salus "Da Franco"

Campo Santa Margherita,
Dorsoduro 3112

Recommended for the younger age range, it is very popular with students from nearby Ca' Foscari University.

Vivaldi

Near Campo S. Polo,
San Polo 1457

Appetisers and local food a stone's throw from Campo San Polo and the church of the same name.

Wine bars

Ai Dogi

Via Andrea Costa 21/i,
Mestre, Tel. 041950707

A rustic, but smart tavern in the old centre, where some of Italy's best labels fight it out with Californian and French wines. Not to mention a fantastic champagne cellar.

Al Leone di San Marco

Via Trezzo 6,
Mestre
Tel. 0415341742

Taste wine at the counter (with an astonishing number of "cicheti") and at table - on the terrace too – where you will be served fish specialities (salt cod, scampi) and Italian and foreign cheeses.

Al Prosecco

Campo San Giacomo
dell'Orio, Santa Croce 1503
Tel. 0415240222

Over 200 labels from every Italian region and from abroad, to sip with local charcuterie and foie gras; even better if you sit out under the plane trees in Venice's only tree-lined piazza.

Al Volto

Calle Cavalli,
San Marco 4081
Tel. 0415228945

Sample the wines and taste excellent "cicheti" just a stone's throw from the newly-reopened La Fenice opera house.

All'Aciugheta

Campo SS. Filippo e Giacomo, Castello 4357
Tel. 0415224292

Plenty of wines to taste with an ample selection of dishes, near the Scuola di San Giorgio degli Schiavoni; if they are on the menu, make sure you taste the mantis

Carneval in Venice

The Venetian carnival dates back to the 10th century and chronicles say that in the days preceding Lent every nationality and class of person amassed in the lanes, attracted by the colourful processions and performances improvised by acrobats and jugglers. Plays were performed everywhere: in coffee shops, theatres and private homes, while the nobles organised magnificent balls in their palaces.

The most important days were Shrove Thursday and Shrove Tuesday. On Thursday the city with corteges of butchers, blacksmiths and craftsmen who led their bulls to Piazza San Marco and in the presence of the Doge, decapitated the animals. Fireworks and the "flight of the angel" followed (nowadays called the "Flight of the Colombina") where an acrobat descended St Mark's belfry down to the Foscara terrace of Palazzo Ducale. Shrove Tuesday is actually the peak of celebrations with costume processions, singing and dancing until midnight.

Even today Carnival in Venice is a great attraction, gathering together thousands of people from all over the world.

Coffee and more

Venice and its theatres

Teatro Grimani a S. Giovanni Grisostomo

Venice has countless theatres, which suffered a decline between 1600 and 1700 since La Serenissima was losing the political importance it had enjoyed for centuries and even its maritime traffic was no longer so intense. All this influenced the state coffers and the patrimonies of the patrician families, many of whom owned theatres.

The *San Cassiano theatre* dates back to the 1500s, belonging to the Tron family of San Benedetto, and it was the most historic, whereas the San Moisé was opened in the late 1600s by the Giustinian family, near Piazza San Marco. The *San Luca* was built in the early 1600s by the Vendramin family of Santa Fosca for comedies and was linked, amongst others, to the name of Carlo Goldoni (who had already worked for the Sant'Angelo theatre), who presented some of his most famous works there, including *Il campiello*, *Gl'innamorati* and the exhilarating *Trilogia della villeggiatura*.

The theatres owned by the Grimani family of Santa Maria Formosa were important since they exercised a sort of monopoly, and three were built during the 17th century: the SS. Giovanni e Paolo theatre (for musical dramas), San Samuele (intended for comedies and competing with the San Luca) and San Giovanni Grisostomo, Venice's biggest.

crab, mussels and anchovies that give the eatery its name.

Il Ghebo
Via Fausta 41,
Località Punta Sabbioni
Cavallino Treporti
Tel. 041658270

At the far end of the Cavallino peninsula, situated in a hotel-restaurant occupying a country house dating from the 1930s, this wine bar offers nearly a thousand kinds of Italian wine from the most famous wine-growing regions; and in addition, the chance to taste local and foreign cheeses as well as other unique dishes.

Mille Vini
San Marco 5362
Tel. 0415206090

Wine-tasting course are also offered in this winery boasting the best

Italian and overseas labels; you can also sample extra-virgin olive oil and purchase gourmet specialities.

Valsugana
Via Miranese 173, Mestre

Great assortment of wines to sample by the glass, accompanied by traditional "cicheti"; all in a rustic, yet cosy ambience.

Vino Vino
Calle delle Veste
S. Marco 2007/a
Tel. 0412417688

A winery that resembles a tavern, where an assortment of wines accompany the menu of the day, chalked up daily on a blackboard (excellent "sarde in saor" and "sepie in trecia").

Patisseries

Da Gilda Vio
Rio Marin 784

The flavours of the past in an old-style pastry shop, where only the finest ingredients are used.

Da Zorzi
Calle dei Fuseri, San Marco 435

Former historic creamery and now famous patisserie, with stylish remodelling and exquisite whipped cream and crème caramel.

Coffee and more

Didovich
Campo San Marina,
Castello 5909
Tel. 0415230017

Near the San Zaccaria church, a patisserie where everything is

handmade, serving traditional pastries but also some original recipes and foreign specialities.

Harry's Dolci alla Giudecca
Fondamenta San Biagio,
Giudecca 773; tel. 0415224844

Out on Giudecca, a "branch office" of the famous Harry's Bar, a must if you have a sweet tooth, but only from April to October. You can also lunch or dine here, with a splendid view over the canal.

Tonolo
Dorsoduro 3764
Tel. 0415237209

Sample some mignon pastries (magnificent cream éclairs) but also cakes, with a coffee on the alternative route from the railway station to Ca' Foscari.

Theatres

Gran Teatro La Fenice
Campo San Fantin 1966
Tel. 0415283780
www.teatrolafenice.it

The opera house destroyed by a blaze in '96 was rebuilt and inaugu-

rated in December 2003. The theatre can be visited accompanied by guides speaking various languages *(tel. 0412424)*.

Teatro Fondamenta Nuove
Cannaregio 5013
Tel. 0415224498
www.teatrofondamentanuove.it

One of the most prestigious and lively Venetian stages, especially interesting for avant-garde dance and theatre.

Coffee and more

Evening gowns for ladies and jacket and tie for men (dinner jackets preferred) are indispensable if you want to enter the Municipal Casino in Venice, which alternated between the summer premises at the Lido and the winter location at Cannaregio until 2002. The Lido venue has now been closed so anyone seeking the thrill of duelling with fortune and has no money worries, now has to "make do" with Palazzo Vendramin Calergi, a magnificent 15th-century building by Mauro Codussi, in Renaissance style laid out around a handsome court decorated with an 11th-century well-curb. If you don't have the right outfit with you or if you prefer not to tempt fortune (all games are played at the casino, from roulette to blackjack and chemin-de-fer), just enjoy the exterior, particularly enchanting in the evening when the building prospect that faces the

Grand Canal is lit to enhance the design of the three floors, set with half columns and cadenced with two-light Gothic windows.

Teatro Goldoni

Calle Teatro Goldoni
San Marco 4650/b
Tel. 0412402011-2402014
www.teatrostabileveneto.it

"Heir" to the historic San Luca theatre, staging many opening nights of comedies by Venice's famous playwright.

Teatro Malibran

Cannaregio 5873
Tel. 041786601
www.teatrolafenice.it

One of the most historic in the city, opened in 1678 under the name of Teatro di San Giovanni Grisostomo. Presents the theatre programme of the Fenice.

Vivaldi's Venice

Not everyone will realise that in Venice, along the Riva degli Schiavoni that tourists march along in crowds as far as the Arsenal, there is a church linked to Antonio Vivaldi, the famous "red priest" who composed the now almost hackneyed *Four Seasons*. It is the Pietà church *(open only during events)*, which you can find on the corner of Rio dei Greci, and founded in the 16th century by Venice's major orphanage (one of the first orphanages in the world), where the musician taught abandoned children for several years. Its educational use was also one of the reasons why the church was rebuilt in the 18th century to an oval plan, to favour acoustics, with the entrance atrium to isolate from outside noise. This is why the church has been used as a concert hall for years, where you will see not only virtuoso en-

semble performers, but also groups in 18th-century costume (many are known as Vivaldi's "Putte" and "Le Venexiane"); even if you are not a great classical music fan, it is worth going to a concert which endows Giambattista Tiepolo's Coronation of Mary fresco with even greater charm, if possible.

The day trip to the Lagoon city has become popular even from quite distant locations like Turin, Genoa, Ancona or Florence and is a direct consequence of the high cost of hotels and guest houses, due to heavy demands (you do need to book a long way ahead) and the presence of foreign tourists with strong currencies. There is little point in pretending that a weekend in Venice will not now cost, on average, the same as a whole week at the Italian coast. It is mainly the hotels that shore up this unenviable reputation: not just those of world fame like the Danieli, Gritti or Cipriani, favoured by VIPs and the international jet set; but the so-called 3-star sector also charges hundreds of euros for service and ambience that are only average quality. Nor is the phenomenon limited to the actual historic centre, or the specific San Marco and San Polo districts, and the Lido, but also secluded areas of Cannaregio or Dorsoduro, or Mestre and Cavallino, who are heading in the same direction thanks to the involvement of big international chains.

Nevertheless, for those who can afford it, a night at the Hotel Danieli, located in Palazzo Dandolo on the Riva degli Schiavoni, has lost none of its magic, and the same can be said for stays at the Cipriani on Giudecca, just a few minutes from San Marco by motor boat, but deeply peaceful and with stunning views of Punta della Dogana and the island of San Giorgio, or a holiday at Hotel Des Bains on the Lido, where you can still enjoy that Middle-European aura that was its hallmark from the WWI period. Yet you can wake up in any number of equally charming hotels – a great many now that charm is in increasing demand in an art city like Venice – that are installed in unknown patrician palaces, retaining their historic stuccoes and furnishings. Try having breakfast in the inner court of a 1300-1400s building, complete with well-curb and with pots of flourishing ivy and other plants, or relaxing after a day amongst the great masterpieces with an aperitif sipped in a lounge furnished with ultra modern, hi-tech sofas, or stay in a pensione or locanda whose past guests may even have included the likes of Lord Byron.

On the other hand, if you are on a tight budget, you have two alternatives: the youth hostel on Giudecca, literally besieged by foreigners almost all year round, or you can try the campsites at Cavallino Treporti, open from Easter to October.

5 stars luxury and	
5 stars	over 200 €
4 stars	100–200 €
3 stars	50–100 €
2 stars	up to 50 €

Hotels

5 stars luxury

Danieli
*Riva degli Schiavoni,
Castello 4196
Tel. 041522648,
fax 0415200208
www.hoteldanielivenice.com*

This hotel needs no introduction and offers its guests accommodation furnished with exquisite elegance and private motor boat service for the Lagoon.

Gritti Palace
*Campo Santa Maria del Giglio,
San Marco 2467
Tel. 041794611-5226044,
fax 0415200942
www.luxurycollection.com*

Sophistication and class in a 17th-century building with rooms overlooking the Grand Canal.

Westin Excelsior
*Lungomare Marconi 41, Lido
Tel. 0415260201,
fax 0415267276
www.westin.com*

In Moorish architecture, this hotel is one of the Lido's exclusive icons, with refined elegance and the loveliest beach on the island.

5 stars

Bauer
*Campo San Moisè,
San Marco 1459
Tel. 0415207022,
fax 0415207557
www.bauervenezia.com*

Magnificent position and equally magnificent, elegant building, both for rooms and furnishings.

When Venice was a "seaside resort"

For a brief but glorious period, the Lido island, separating the Lagoon from the Adriatic, was one of the most elite holiday resorts on the Old Continent. For about sixty years, Middle Europe's rich aristocracy preferred to spend time relaxing in one of various eclectic Art Nouveau hotels that from the 1850s onwards were built on a strip of land that until then had been virtually deserted. It was certainly a splendid time for part of Venice, where the sandy beaches offered literati and poets endless vistas of the Adriatic, while the inhabitants of the Austro-Hungarian and German empires discovered the therapeutic effects of sea and sunbathing on aching bones full of rheumatism. This glittering history has left chiefly a heritage of Art Nouveau, Art deco and 1930s hotels, with one or two 1920s constructions, for tourism has now shifted its attention from the Lido's flat stretch-

es of flourishing green to rather more exotic and distant destinations. Nevertheless, when you alight from the water-bus you will be struck by the elegance of Lido's historic structure, which did not acquire residential buildings until the post-World War II period, to meet overflow from Venice itself. The main street is Gran Viale Santa Maria Elisabetta, where you will find lots of 19th-20th century architectures, closing at Piazzale Bucintoro. Other buildings of that era are on the Lungomare Guglielmo Marconi, where you will easily find the Grand Hotel des Bains (early 20th century), the Film Festival building with the old casino next door (both 1920s architecture) and the Hotel Excelsior opposite, and the first to be built (1898-1908) for Middle European guests.

Hotels

Luna Baglioni
Calle larga dell'Ascensione,
San Marco 1243
Tel. 0415289840,
fax 0415287160
www.baglionihotels.com

Frescoes by the Tiepolo
school make the interior
even more precious, fur-
nished with 18th-centu-
ry items.

Grand Hotel dei Dogi
Fondamenta Madonna
dell'Orto, Cannaregio 3500
Tel. 0412208111,
fax 041722278
www.boscolo.com/hotels

A view over the north-
ern Lagoon from a hotel
in a historic palazzo
with an inner garden.

4 stars

Amadeus
Rio Terrà Lista di Spagna,
Cannaregio 227
Tel. 0412206000,
fax 0412206020
www.bestwestern.it

Rooms with period
furniture.

Ambasciatori
Corso del Popolo 221, Mestre
Tel. 0415310699,
fax 0415310074
www.ambasciatori.it

Although its target is
business tourism, its po-
sition behind the rail-
way station makes it
ideal if you don't mind
commuting into Venice
over the lagoon bridge.

BELLINI
OSCOLO FIRST CLASS HOTEL

Bellini
Rio Terrà Lista di Spagna,
Cannaregio 116/119
Tel. 0415242488,
fax 041715193
www.boscolohotels.com

Although it is at the be-
ginning of the street
connecting the railway
station to Rialto, it does
boast a quiet position
and is comfortable.

Biasutti
Via Dandolo 27/29, Lido
Tel. 0415260120,
fax 0415261259
www.bestwestern.it

A fascinating location in
three historic villas, hidden in the Lido's oldest
quarter amidst lovely
gardens.

Carlton
& Grand Canal
Santa Croce 578
Tel. 0412752200,
fax 0412752250
www.carltongrandcanal.com

A typical Venetian
palazzo offering sig-
nificant levels of service
and comfortable
interiors.

Cavalletto e
Doge Orseolo
Calle del Cavalletto,
San Marco 1107
Tel. 0415200955,
fax 0415238184
www.sanmarcohotels.com

The rooms in the main
building are the nicest,
in Venetian
style, with
view
over the
Grand
Canal.

Cipriani
Fondamenta San Giovanni,
Giudecca 10
Tel. 0415207744,
fax 0415203930
www.hotelcipriani.it

Peace and seclusion
just a two-minute
motor-boat ride from
Piazza San Marco, with
meticulously well-kept
rooms, even in the
marvellous annexes,
which are all installed
in other historic
buildings.

Concordia
Calle larga San Marco,
San Marco 367
Tel. 0415206866,
fax 0415206775
www.hotelconcordia.it

If you want to take in
all of Piazza San Marco
from your room, you
will have to book an
elegant room in this
hotel.

Des Bains
Lungomare Marconi 17, Lido
Tel. 0415265921,
fax 0415260113
www.sheraton.com

Another Lido icon
is this Art Nouveau
hotel where Thomas
Mann set his Death in
Venice; sumptuous,
elegant interiors,
breathtaking terrace
with sea view.

Hotels

Europa & Regina
Corte Barozzi,
San Marco 2159
Tel. 0412400001,
fax 0415231533
www.westin.com

If you are fond of the Salute basilica, a hotel with a view from San Marco, with spacious, comfortable rooms.

Gabrielli Sandwirth
Riva degli Schiavoni,
Castello 4110
Tel. 0415231580,
fax 0415209455
http://gabrielli.hotelinvenice.com

A 15th-century palazzo that tempts guests with breakfast served in the dining room and a terrace view.

Giorgione
Campo SS. Apostoli,
Cannaregio 4587
Tel. 0415225810,
fax 0415239092
www.hotelgiorgione.com

Attention to detail and great service that is never intrusive, in a hotel with well-furnished rooms.

Le Boulevard
Gran Viale
S. Maria Elisabetta 41, Lido
Tel. 0415361990,
fax 0415261917
www.leboulevard.com

A 1930s building in the style of the Film Festival's early period.

Londra Palace
Riva degli Schiavoni,
Castello 4171
Tel. 0415200533,
fax 0415225032
www.hotellondra.it

HOTEL MONACO & GRAND CANA

Tchaikovsky composed his Fourth Symphony in this hotel, overlooking the Grand Canal, with period furniture in all the rooms.

Metropole
Riva degli Schiavoni,
Castello 4149
Tel. 0415205044,
fax 0415223679
www.hotelmetropole.com

A building whose garden is decorated with

an authentic well-curb and the rooms are furnished with antiques.

Michelangelo
Via Forte Marghera 69,
Mestre
Tel. 041986664-986600,
fax 041986052

A garden with centuries-old trees in the centre of town, concealing a welcoming and quiet building, ideal for anyone

who wants to relax as well as visit Venice.

Monaco & Grand Canal
Calle Vallaresso,
San Marco 1332
Tel. 0415200211,
fax 0415200501
www.hotelmonaco.it

Ideal for visiting Venice especially for those who prefer the Punta della Dogana to the rest of the city, with a view from welcoming, well-kept rooms.

Palazzo del Giglio
Campo Santa Maria del Giglio,
San Marco 2462
Tel. 0412719111,
fax 0415205158
www.hotelgiglio.com

If you like period buildings and unusual ambience, all furnished with antiques, of course.

Quattro Fontane
Via delle Quattro Fontane 16, Lido
Tel. 0415260227,
fax 0415260726
www.quattrofontane.com

Period furniture, packed bookshelves and unusual collections make this hotel, set in a park near the beach, an ideal holiday location.

Saturnia & International
Calle larga XXII Marzo,
San Marco 2398
Tel. 0415208377-5236137,
fax 0415207131
www.hotelsaturnia.it

The elegant 14th-century building, with a magnificent terrace on the top floor and rooms with classic antique furniture.

Villa Mabapa
Riviera San Nicolò 16, Lido
Tel. 0415260590,
fax 0415269441
www.villamabapa.com

A 1930s villa that is really popular with golfers (there is a golf course nearby) and has very comfortable rooms.

3 stars

Accademia Villa Maravege
Fondamenta Bollani,
Dorsoduro 1058
Tel. 0415210188-0415237846,
fax 0415239152
www.pensioneaccademia.it

A historic villa with gardens and period furnishings in all the rooms.

Ariston
Via Bergamo 12, Mestre
Tel. 041985577,
fax 041972293
www.hotelaristonvenice.com

Not in the centre but well-connected with Venice and offering cosy rooms.

Atlanta Augustus
Via Lepanto 15, Lido
Tel. 0415260569,
fax 0415265604
www.hotelatlanta.it

An Art Nouveau villa furnished in Venetian style, in a street off the main thoroughfare.

Bonvecchiati
Calle Goldoni,
San Marco 4488
Tel. 0415285017,
fax 0415285230
www.hotelinvenice.it

Venetian-style rooms, marble bathrooms, elegant reception rooms in a hotel that has refurbished a 19th-century building.

Do Pozzi
Calle larga XXII Marzo
S. Marco 2373
Tel. 0415207855,
fax 0415229413
www.hoteldopozzi.it

In the "campiello" where in summer you can breakfast by the two well-curbs that give the hotel its name; comfortable, minimal rooms.

Garibaldi
Viale Garibaldi 24, Mestre
Tel. 0415349362,
fax 0415347565
www.hotelgaribaldi.it

In a strategic position for anyone visiting Venice who can't afford local hotel prices, and popular because of its quite secluded position.

Helvetia
Gran Viale S. Maria Elisabetta
4/6, Lido; tel. 0415260105,
fax 0415268403
www.hotelhelvetia.com

Greets visitors arriving by ferry: the historic business has reception rooms furnished in the Venetian style.

La Calcina
Zattere, Dorsoduro 780
Tel. 0415206466,
fax 0415227045
www.lacalcina.com

Family-run business for a hotel that offers meticulous service and has a terrace overlooking the Giudecca canal.

La Fenice et des Artistes
Campiello della Fenice,
San Marco 1936
Tel. 0415232333,
fax 0415203721
www.fenicehotels.it

Located in the same square as Venice's

most famous theatre so it was a favourite with the performers; lovely inner gardens and rooms with period furniture.

La Meridiana
Via Lepanto 45, Lido
Tel. 0415260343,
fax 0415269240
www.lameridiana.com

A simple hotel in a 1930s building, offering bed and breakfast.

Locanda Sturion
Calle dello Sturion,
San Polo 679
Tel. 0415236243,
fax 0415228378
www.locandasturion.com

Use this hotel if you want to breathe some Venetian history: it is very old and has simple rooms.

Marconi
Riva del Vin,
San Polo 729
Tel. 0415222068,
fax 0415229700
www.hotelmarconi.it

Venetian-style, with cosy rooms near the Rialto Bridge.

Montecarlo
Calle degli Specchieri,
San Marco 463
Tel. 0415207144,
fax 0415207789
www.venicehotelmontecarlo.com

A hotel with Venetian-style furnishings and prompt, courteous service.

Olimpia
Fondamenta delle Burchielle,
Santa Croce 395
Tel. 041711041, fax
0415246777
www.hotel-olimpia.com

Lacquered furniture and toning fabrics in a hotel where hospitality is a prime concern.

Panada
Calle degli Specchieri,
S. Marco 646; tel. 0415209088,
fax 0415209619
www.hotelpanada.com

A restructured 18th-century palazzo with rooms in Venetian style.

Pausania
Fondamenta Gherardini,
Dorsoduro 2824
Tel. 0415222083,
fax 0415222989
www.hotelpausania.it

A patrician house with front courtyard and a veranda opening onto the charming inner court.

Piave
Via Col Moschin 6/10, Mestre
Tel. 041929477, fax 041929651
www.3starshotel.it

Try and book the annex rooms, located in a late 19th-century villa subjected to an excellent restoration.

Rialto
Riva del Ferro, San Marco 5149
Tel. 0415209166,
fax 0415238958
www.rialtohotel.com

A stone's throw from the Rialto Bridge, with some rooms in Venetian style.

Riviera
Gran Viale Santa Maria
Elisabetta 5, Lido,
Tel. 0415260031-5260444,
fax 0415265979
www.rivieravenezia.it

In a typical Venetian-style red building, this hotel offers a splendid view of the city and has surprising period furniture rooms.

San Cassiano
Calle della Rosa, S. Croce 2232
Tel. 0415241768, fax 04172103
www.sancassiano.it

In a 15th-century palazzo overlooking the Grand Canal, its hallmark is the small terrace that seems to float over the water.

San Moisè
Piscina San Moisè, San Marco
2058, Tel. 0415203755,
fax 0415210670
www.sanmoise.it

Antique mirrors, Murano chandeliers and original parquet are just some of